Cameron's Raid

Cameron's Raid

Philip McCutchan

Weidenfeld and Nicolson
London

Published in Great Britain by
George Weidenfeld & Nicolson Limited
91 Clapham High Street
London sw4 7TA

ISBN 0 297 78517 6

Typeset at The Spartan Press Limited
Lymington Hants
Printed in Great Britain by
Butler & Tanner Ltd,
Frome and London

1

The draft had left from the barracks siding at 0630 hours that morning, in the aftermath of an air raid over Portsmouth. Fires were burning still as the train pulled through the Town Station and chuffed on steamily for Fratton. A pall of smoke hung; it could be smelled strongly as it wafted into the carriages even though all the windows had been hauled tight shut on their leather straps to keep out a bitter winter dawn. Snow lay fairly thick; there could be points trouble, Chief Petty Officer Tiny King thought, knowing the ways of the Southern Railway. Thank God the line to Cardiff hadn't been electrified like the London line to Waterloo . . . the steam engines could usually pull a train out of anything, though even they might well be defeated by frozen points, of course. And they had a long way to go. Tiny King, a large man, projected his thoughts ahead and at the same time astern. Seventy-eight ratings – seamen and stokers plus signalmen, telegraphists and a crowd of cooks, stewards and supply assistants collectively known to the Navy as miscellaneous. Tiny King rubbed his nose reflectively. For the best part of a week now the barracks tannoy had been busy, calling far too often for the party now entrained.

'Do you hear there . . . all ratings detailed Party Scatter muster outside the Drafting Master-at-Arms' office . . . all ratings detailed Party Scatter muster at the sick bay . . . all ratings detailed Party Scatter muster with pay books outside the pay office . . .'

On and on and on. Bugger Party Scatter, King thought

irritably, it had come between him and his leave and God alone knew when he'd be back in Pompey to take it. He shifted a little as his mate Chief Petty Officer Bartlett came away from the carriage window and sat down heavily alongside him. Bartlett was looking sombre – they all were.

'Thoughts of home, eh?' King said sympathetically.

'That's right.' Bartlett lived in Pompey, not far from the prison which they'd just passed on their right. 'The missus is getting past taking this sort of thing. Had enough of being left on her own before the war, more than enough I reckon.'

King nodded. Bartlett was a Royal Fleet Reservist, called back to the service in September 1939 after being out some years on pension. It was harder on the old buffers . . . King himself was seven years younger and hadn't yet taken his pension – he was what was known as active service, this being no more than a way of distinguishing between those like himself and the others – the RFR men and the hostilities-only ratings of which the service was now made up of around ninety per cent.

The train pulled on through Cosham, heading for South-ampton, Salisbury and the west.

Bartlett said, for the hundredth time, 'Wonder what it's all in aid of.'

'We'll know soon enough, Barty.'

'Bet they don't even tell us when we join the bloody ship.'

'Depends on the skipper – and what orders *he*'s got, doesn't it?'

Bartlett nodded. The buzzes had been legion and lurid, most of them daft. They were going to steam up the Elbe in a gunboat and grab hold of bloody Adolf Hitler . . . Sir Stafford Cripps was to be embarked in Cardiff docks and on arrival in Berlin would set up a provisional government in the name of the King of England and the President of the United States. Tripe like that. The war had not been going quite so well for Hitler, not after Rommel had been chased out of North Africa by Monty, and the Führer just might be in a settling mood, said that particular buzz. Others said it was

2

more convoy work, heaving around the North Atlantic or freezing their bollocks off on the icy Murmansk run. Neither King nor Bartlett believed that. You didn't form a special party like Party Scatter, give it a name and all, just for a routine draft. Another buzz had insisted they were going to do a cutting-out job, not Hitler, but General de Gaulle – cut him out, that was, from England and dump him back in his beloved France, whereupon, it was said, Winston Churchill would heave an almighty sigh of relief. All these rumours sprang, as they always did, from very authoritative sources such as the wardroom pantry staff or the Commodore's steward, all men with big, flapping ears and a devilish desire to fool the gullible. The ungullible used their common sense, disregarded the buzzes and settled for something bloody dangerous from which they might or might not come back to enjoy the blessings of the land . . . war was war and it had been going on for too long already. War had become a way of life; you rolled and pitched around the oceans and got shot at, or bombed, or torpedoed, and you took leave when it was given and then back to more bloodshed and discomfort along the messdecks, dressed for the most part in any old rubbish that would keep you from freezing if you were in northern waters, and practically sod all if you were in a hot climate. Nobody thought any more now about the good old peacetime days of the Home and Mediterranean Fleets, all the drills and manoeuvres and runs ashore in tiddley uniforms, lanyards and all for those 'dressed as seamen' which was officialese for bell-bottoms. It was a different world now. So many of the stately big ships had gone too: *Hood, Prince of Wales, Repulse, Royal Oak, Barham* . . . and so many old shipmates.

They stopped at a station and were ordered out for refreshments. It had all been laid on in a waiting-room manned by ladies of the wvs. Half an hour's halt and then they moved on again, going slow on account of bomb damage further along the line. Goering's Luftwaffe played continual hell with the railway timetables. When they reached Cardiff the winter evening was almost upon them. In a cloud of steam

King, in charge of the draft, got down on to the platform and shouted for the bags and hammocks to be got out double quick. The platform became piled. In the middle of it all King was approached by a Railway Transport Officer wearing the badges of the South Wales Borderers.

King saluted.

'Party Scatter?' the Major asked. 'Which depot are you?'

'Pompey, sir. I – '

'You're in charge? Right. You're going on to Barry docks. Train'll be in shortly. All right?'

'Well, I suppose it has to be, sir. Why Barry, sir?'

The Major shrugged. 'Don't ask me. You'll find out when you get there. D'you know your ship?'

'No, I don't, sir. I – '

'Party Scatter from Portsmouth.' The RTO shuffled some papers clipped to a board. 'You're detailed for HMS *Palatine*. Does that convey anything to you, Chief?'

King said bitterly, 'It does an' all, sir.'

'Right, fine. Embark your men as soon as the train pulls in.'

King saluted an already turned back; the officers of Railway Transport were busy men from time to time. Busy but comfortable: they didn't have to go to sea. King walked down the platform for a word with Bartlett, angry that it had been left to the brown jobs to pass their orders.

'*Palatine*,' he said shortly.

Bartlett swore. 'The P boats . . . bloody older than the old V and Ws!'

King shrugged. 'We might have guessed it had to be a destroyer. You and me, we've both done our time in the boats.'

'Yes. I wonder what it is this time.'

King said, 'Something bloody nasty.' He was thinking to himself that the P class destroyers were just about the most expendable you could get. They were nearly as old as the 'packets of Woodbines', the four-stackers bought from the US Navy on a cash-and-carry basis, fifty of them that had proved their worth on convoy escort duties but almost shook to

4

pieces every time they went to sea. In them, you really earned your hard-lying money. King whistled softly through set teeth. A lousy draft and now, being South Wales, it was raining. It felt as though it might turn to snow at any moment. It was being driven into their faces by a biting wind that blasted across the platform beneath the canopy. The kitbags and hammocks were in for a soaking if the Barry train didn't pull its socks up. And why Barry? Coal dust and more rain . . . Barry dock was a coal port, best quality Welsh coal from the valleys, responsible for all the slag heaps that had turned the green valleys to gloom and squalor. But – as King now remembered – war had brought changes to Barry dock. Barry Roads was now a convoy assembly point and Barry dock was one of the bases of the Naval Control Service that gave the masters and escorts their orders and safe – theoretically safe – routes.

It began to look like a routine convoy job after all; but somehow Chief Petty Officer King still didn't believe it was.

And seven miles to the south-west, in Barry on the Bristol Channel, Lieutenant-Commander Cameron, who was to command HM destroyer *Palatine* in her old age and had been standing by her for the past week, now knew for certain that it was not. Beneath heavier rain than that falling on Cardiff, a rain that seemed to blacken everything rather than wash it, as though it was bringing down from the skies its measure of good Welsh coal-dust, he had walked from the Barry Hotel to the headquarters of the Naval Officer In Charge, Captain Sir Ralph Crooke, RN. There he had been given his orders and had at the same time been sworn to secrecy. Not a word was to be breathed to anyone at all until the *Palatine* and two of her sister ships – *Probity* and *Panoply*, whose commanding officers were also in attendance – had left both the port and the Bristol Channel. After that – after they had left Lundy Island astern in company with a convoy of sixty-three ships bound through for Dover – then and only then could the commanding officers take their ships' companies into their confidence. The senior officer of Party Scatter, Crooke said,

5

would be in *Panoply*, manned by another group of Party Scatter from the RN Barracks at Devonport; *Probity* would take a draft from Chatham, and all three ships would embark parties of Royal Marine Commandos from Eastney and Deal. These commando parties would arrive next day in closed transport which would be driven straight into the docks and alongside the three destroyers.

When the briefing was over NOIC nodded dismissals at the Captains of *Panoply* and *Probity*. Cameron, possibly because he was the only RNVR commanding officer in the small group, was retained for a personal pep talk. 'I need hardly tell you, there's immense danger in this,' Crooke said, 'but it's a very vital job and it must be brought off successfully, simply must.' He pulled at his chin, a mannerism Cameron had observed before – Captain Crooke, not having been provided with an official quarter of his own, lived as the other officers did in the Barry Hotel. 'I've been acquainted with your record – it's a good one. I have every confidence you'll do your best, Cameron.'

'Thank you, sir. I shall.'

Crooke nodded. He went on, 'You'll have two more nights in the hotel before the convoy leaves – the fitting-out will not be finished as regards the accommodation until shortly before sailing. Dock workers . . . civilians.' He was disparaging. 'I suggest you don't in any way . . . er . . . drown your worries for the future, a habit of younger officers I fear. Alcohol leads to loose tongues . . . and thick heads. You will warn your own officers that thick heads will not be tolerated.'

'Yes, sir.' Cameron met the Captain's eye. He knew of him by reputation. A dry stick, withdrawn and aloof, inclined to fuss, a very old man still to be serving. He had first been a captain in the days before the Great War, had been at Jutland and had later commanded the Gunnery School at Whale Island. He had retired in the early thirties as a full admiral and on the outbreak of the present war he had returned to the service as Commodore RNR before reverting to the RN rank of Captain. He was one of the old Navy, so old that he looked as

6

though he might crumble away at any moment. Cameron said, 'I'll ensure that everyone's fit, sir.'

'Good! They need to be, I'm sure you appreciate that. That's all, Cameron.'

Cameron left NOIC's office and walked back through the rain to the Barry Hotel almost opposite the railway station. There was time for a drink before dinner but, bearing in mind NOIC's cautionary words, he refrained from having even one gin. There probably wouldn't in fact be any, which was one consolation; spirits were almost unobtainable ashore and he didn't feel like Brain's beer. He went into the lounge, where Archer was waiting and doing the *Daily Telegraph* crossword – the quick one. Lieutenant Archer, who was to be Cameron's First Lieutenant, was no intellectual.

He looked up at Cameron's approach and got to his feet. He was tall and thin and tended to gangle. He grinned amiably and said, 'You look chokker, sir. Bad news?'

Cameron said, 'Yes. NOIC's taken a dislike to strong drink. Pass the word, please, Number One.'

'Is this an order?'

'Not precisely. Just a word of warning. Clear heads are going to be needed. As to the rest of the news . . . that will have to wait.'

Archer confirmed Cameron's earlier reflections. 'There's no gin or whisky anyway. The hardships of NOIC are not great. Anyway – I'll pass the word, sir. There's probably beer, even if only for the commercial travellers in the downstairs bar.'

Cameron nodded and went to his room for a wash. The lounge had been full of Naval officers: it was just like any wardroom. Naval Control Service officers, mostly RNR, NOIC's staff, and others visiting from the convoy escorts in the docks. The hotel seemed to have been virtually taken over and the commercial gentry had been scared off by the preponderance of gold braid. Perhaps they thought there was a danger of being shanghaied. Leaving his room for dinner, Cameron passed the hotel manager.

'Good evening, Mr Rees.'

'Ah, Commander – good evening to you.' Rees, a stout man, seemed breathless. 'Perhaps you can tell me, can you, how long you will be staying, Commander, you and the other officers?'

'Sorry, Mr Rees. I'll let you know as soon as I can.'

The manager went off, looking harrassed. Careless Talk Costs Lives . . . much, perhaps, could be gleanable to spying ears from any advance information as to when the officers of the three destroyers were checking out. By such scraps could the sailing dates of vital convoys be pieced together. Frankly, Cameron would be glad to get back aboard a ship; meanwhile *Panoply*, *Palatine* and *Probity* were being fitted out for their task and were currently uninhabitable as NOIC had remarked. At dinner Cameron sat at a long table with his First Lieutenant and navigator and the captains of the other two ships detailed for what was about to become Operation Scatter. The other officers were either living it up – not too vividly, Cameron hoped – in Cardiff or were on duty aboard their ships. Half-way through dinner – a wartime austerity feast of brown Windsor soup, some unidentifiable meat with a couple of potatoes and some tinned peas – Cameron's gunner, Mr Cantley RN, came in and before sitting down made a report.

'Ship's company joined, sir, under the 'swain and buffer – names o' King and Bartlett.'

'Know them, do you, Guns?'

'No. I've sailed with the gunner's mate, Jack Todd. He's a good hand. As to the ship's company – duty watch aboard, kip down where they can. Remainder marched to the Sally Army. As arranged, sir. All right, sir?'

Cameron nodded. 'Bring your arse to an anchor, Guns, and enjoy the good things of life while you can.'

An unintentional slip? Cantley's sharp ears seemed to have caught something and he met Cameron's eye. Cameron gave a cough and shifted target. His glance rested for a moment on Captain Sir Ralph and Lady Crooke. They were not speaking to each other; Lady Crooke was looking around with a

8

commanding eye and not liking what she had to dine with: nearly all reserves. The Captain was examining his personal butter dish as if suspecting nefarious hotel staff of raiding his ration. Mr Cantley sat down and drank soup. His expression said, good things of life be buggered, and sod the exigencies of shoreside wartime grub. Mr Cantley liked plenty of good Scotch beef; his ruddy complexion bore witness to the fact of much eaten in the past. He had built up a kind of reserve, which was fortunate.

In the Salvation Army hostel King and Bartlett and the gunner's mate, Petty Officer Todd, sorted out the sleeping billets and then went out in search of beer. They might as well, Todd said, have a skinful that would likely have to last. They were all in a subdued mood that even the beer didn't lift. They were all thinking of home; no one was ever easy under unknown orders. Once they knew, all would be different.

2

During the night the drafts came in from
Devonport and Chatham, the ships' companies for *Panoply*
and *Probity*. The Salvation Army hostel became a crowded
place and from time to time heard unaccustomed blasphemy
as the ratings searched for free space on the floor. But the
shore gangs had been working through the night and by the
next day the accommodation was more or less ready to
receive the men and they were marched aboard during the
afternoon watch. In the last dog-watch the Royal Marines
arrived with buttoned-up lips in their transport; and the
messdecks, despite a considerable reduction in the normal
size of the ships' companies, became as tightly packed as the
Salvation Army.

Even before he'd been told about the commandos, Tiny
King, who had spent the day working with Bartlett and the
gunner's mate on the watch and quarter bill, the summary of
every man's station for the various situations of action, two-
and three-watch systems, fire, abandon ship and a number of
other contingencies, had been formulating some ideas. He
had found the reduced complement significant. No one back
at RNB had enlightened him and his expectation had been that
Palatine already had a nucleus aboard.

But not so.

'Know what?' he asked the gunner's mate.

'What, 'Swain?'

'Special mission. No doubt about it now.'

'Like what, eh?' The gunner's mate stared at him. He had

had similiar thoughts. He voiced them before King did. 'Hitler's perishing France?'

'Could be,' King agreed. 'Stands to reason.'

'What does?'

King shrugged. 'Wouldn't want to lose unnecessary hands. You don't need a full complement of matloes for a short trip, do you? And then there's them bootnecks,' he added in reference to the marines.

Neither of them knew how right they were. Petty Officer Todd asked if there were any buzzes as to when they were leaving. King said, 'Convoy's still forming up. I reckon it'll be tomorrow night.'

Todd lit a cigarette, handed the packet to the coxswain. He said briefly. 'Time to write a letter.'

'Yes.' Once again their thoughts had swung homeward. PO Todd, gunner's mate, active service and in line for chief, was another who lived in Pompey, off Lake Road in North End. There had been too many Jerry bombs around that part already. If *Palatine*'s guns, his guns, could do anything to stop bloody Hitler in his tracks, he would be happy enough to see it. Hitler, via Goering, had turned his missus into a nervous wreck; he was dead worried about her. Done his best to get her out of Pompey but would she go? Would she hell! No parents, no more had he, and nowhere familiar to go. Despite the shakes, she had guts, Lucy had. Suddenly Todd, who had never been all that keen on starting a family, wished he'd had a son. Someone to carry on, someone to support Lucy if he didn't come back. Didn't come back this time . . . every trip to sea could have been the last but it hadn't really struck home till now.

He got to his feet. 'Want me any more, 'Swain?'

'No, that's all right, Jack.'

'Right. I'll take a look round the guns. Before Cantley does.'

King looked up from his pencil work – Watch and Quarter Bills were, in the early stages anyway, a matter of rubbing out. Gunner's party, parts of watches, duty hands, Quarters

Clean Guns and all that, it was half jigsaw, half bird's nest. He asked. 'What's he like, Jack? Know him, you said.'

'Yes. Cantley's all right,' Todd answered briefly. 'Just so long as there's no slackness.'

He went off, going out on deck, avoiding Royal Marines in khaki battledress and carrying rifles and packs. They were everywhere. Todd went for'ard, along the fo'c'sle, right up to the eyes of the ship. It was a pointless journey, really: too ruddy dark to take a look at the guns. What he'd really wanted was to get out on deck, never mind the mist now coming up across the breakwater – he could feel it on his bare skin and he could smell it too. Might cause delay if it persisted. He thought about the armament. Two 4-inch guns before the bridge, with two more aft. Amidships a high-angle gun that had seen better days a long while before. The only modern stuff was around the forebridge, close-range weapons – Oerlikons – and just for'ard of the searchlight platform there was a multiple pom-pom. The old crap heap had once had torpedo tubes, six of them in triple mountings, but they'd been removed on the outbreak of war, God knew why. Her depth charges were intact, in the racks and throwers aft, pistols withdrawn whilst in harbour. As Todd moved aft toward the break of the fo'c'sle he saw someone coming up the starboard ladder alongside the bridge.

Mr Cantley.

'Evening, Todd.'

'Good evening, sir.'

'It's not half a dirty night, eh.' Cantley shivered; he'd come out on deck without an oilskin or duffel-coat, in a deplorable old uniform monkey-jacket from which the single thin gold stripe of his warrant rank hung half off on one sleeve. He grinned in the darkness. 'Like me, aren't you, Jack?'

'How's that, then?'

'Can't keep away from 'em – the guns. Potty stuff for these days . . . but we mustn't criticize, eh? Poor buggers might hear and get disheartened before they start.'

'They might at that.' Todd paused. 'Any buzzes, sir?'

Cantley said, 'Come off it, you know better than to ask me that. I don't know any more'n you do.' He became formal. 'One thing: I want a full run through tomorrow forenoon. Full gun drill, get the crews working together and make sure nothing's going to fall apart. See to that, all right?'

'Aye, aye, sir.'

'I'll check with Number One first, but you can assume it'll be right after Both Watches. And one more thing: a cat.'

'*Cat*?'

'Yes, cat. Ship's got no bloody cat that I've seen so far. Can't have that. Send one of your party ashore first thing, scavenge for a cat.'

'Shanghai the poor bloody beast?'

'It won't mind. Most of the dockside cats'll have done more sea-time than you have, Jack. Promise it four square meals a day.'

'Very good, sir.' Todd's tone was ironic. 'Any particular preference, have you?'

Cantley hadn't. He took a turn around the fo'c'sle, then walked aft along the iron-deck with his gunner's mate. When Cantley had gone below to the wardroom, Todd reflected on cats. Didn't seem fair to take a cat, willy-nilly, into mortal danger: on the other hand most ships did have them. It was a matter of good luck, really. A black cat would be the ticket, of course. Todd went along to the seamen's messdeck, which in fact contained more bootnecks than matloes, and found Leading Seaman Wicks, his right-hand man in the gunner's party. When he passed the order re a cat, Wicks was all for it. He, too, believed in luck. They couldn't sail without a cat.

Early next morning Cameron, walking through to his ship after another night in the Barry Hotel, his cabin not yet being ready, found the cat hunt in progress. A very paunchy able seaman was behaving oddly, tip-toeing around the corner of a weary-looking dockside hut. As an officer came into his field of vision, the able seaman stopped his antics and saluted.

Cameron said, 'Good morning. You're from *Palatine*, aren't you?'

'Yessir. Trudge, sir, AB.'

'I thought I recognized you.' He'd seen Trudge on deck during the first dog-watch the day before. 'May I ask what you're doing, Trudge?'

'Cat, sir. Gunner's mate's orders, sir.' Trudge explained in full.

'Ah! Well, I wish you luck, Trudge. Sooner you than me.' Cameron walked on. Stripey Trudge – Stripey on account of the three red badges on the left sleeve of his Number Three uniform, bearing witness to a minimum of thirteen years' blameless conduct – carried on. There was, or had been, a tabby washing itself in the lee of the hut and it had looked like a fair catch if Stripey Trudge could move fast enough. When he edged once again round the angle of the hut the bloody thing had buggered off. Not his fault; he'd been interrupted at the psychological moment. Officers! Stripey moved off tiredly in search of another victim. There ought to be plenty in Barry, what with all the ships – and anyway he believed the Welsh were fond of cats. Somehow cats seemed to go with the traditional steeple-shaped black hats . . .

Cameron, saluted aboard *Palatine* by the Officer of the Day, an RNR lieutenant named Burton who was also to be his navigator, went to his cabin and tested the paint. Nicely dry. And not long to go now.

A few minutes later Archer tapped at his door and came in.

'Well, Number One. How's it going?'

'All correct, sir.' Archer, who was RN and tended towards a stiff formality on duty, stood rigidly at attention, cap beneath his left arm. Cameron grinned and told him to relax. He didn't, not noticeably; and he rendered a full report. Fuel tanks full, all hands aboard, ship ammunitioned and stored. The marines, under a major, a captain, two lieutenants and a colour-sergeant were uncomfortable but philosophic. 'They seem to have enough weapons for a whole battalion, sir.'

Cameron nodded non-committally. He said, 'Convoy will be fully assembled by 1500 hours. For your private information and Burton's in a moment – we leave at high water.

14

That's at 1535.'

'Yes, sir.' Archer was inclined to linger in the hope of picking up further information, but he was unlucky. Cameron had nothing more to offer. He told Archer to carry on and asked him to send the navigator along. Three minutes later Lieutenant Burton knocked.

'Charts, Pilot. I take it the folio's arrived.'

'Came aboard late last night, sir.'

'You've checked through?'

'Yes, sir – '

'Notice anything?'

Burton frowned uncertainly. 'Not really. Nothing out of the ordinary . . . all corrections entered to date from Notices to Mariners.' He paused, watched by Cameron. 'The folio's the Channel and the North Sea . . . more than the Channel as a matter of fact. Biscay's covered too.'

Cameron nodded. 'All right, Pilot, just checking. You know the convoy's route. South from Lundy, down into the Channel and turn to port off the Wolf Rock and continue past the Lizard.'

'The usual route for Dover. Yes, I know all that, sir. It's all laid off already.'

Once again Cameron nodded. Burton had sounded a little tetchy. As an experienced navigator, an officer with several years' service with P & O, he must know the Channel like the back of his hand. That was obvious. Cameron cursed the need for secrecy; he liked to take his officers into his confidence. Currently he had a brand-new set of officers and he hadn't yet taken their measure nor they his. He had been ham-handed in his query about whether Burton had noticed anything; and he didn't want friction or distrust between him and his navigator. Full co-operation was going to be vital to success, to the lives of everyone aboard – aboard the other two destroyers as well. As it was, there was nothing more he could add. NOIC had been very specific: absolutely nothing was to be said. Not yet. Cameron had just wanted to be sure that there had been no give-away in the fact that the charts for Biscay had been

15

included in the folio. The convoy certainly wasn't going that way. But evidently it hadn't registered with Burton. In point of fact it was common practice to provide a ship with charts of her contiguous areas. He was being too pedantic over this, too fussy. He said, 'All right, Pilot. Thank you. Just have everything on the top line for 1535 this afternoon. That's when we leave.'

'Right, sir.' Burton left the cabin. The day's routine swung into gear. After Both Watches at 0800 Mr Cantley had his gun drill, which went on right through the forenoon. CPO King reported with the First Lieutenant and the Watch and Quarter Bill, which Cameron perused as a formality. If it was all right for Number One, whose responsibility it was, it was all right for him. They wouldn't need it much anyway, not after arrival – from then on it would be all action, and come to that they would be closed up at action stations virtually all the way after clearing from Barry Roads, but you had to go through all the proper motions. During the forenoon that day, together with the OC marine detachment and Lieutenant-Commander Grey, an RNR officer commanding *Probity*, Cameron was sent for to go aboard the leader, *Panoply*, for a conference with the Senior Officer, Captain Farnon. Like Archer and Sir Ralph Crooke, Farnon was RN, but of a different stamp from the latter. Farnon was an easy man, very relaxed, very friendly, with a humorous twist to his mouth and a sensitive face, and young for his rank. For a moment his glance rested on the ribbon of the DSC on Cameron's jacket. He made no reference to it, but it had registered. His own jacket bore a DSO ribbon in addition to the DSC and the medals and stars of the Great War. There was a full discussion of all details of the forthcoming operation; and all the alternatives, should anything go wrong as it well might, were gone into very fully. The destroyer captains were left in no doubt as to how Farnon meant to conduct affairs and in no doubt as to his wishes and orders. It was a long business; Cameron took lunch in Farnon's cabin and the briefing continued into the afternoon. In the meantime other matters

16

had been in hand ashore and Stripey Trudge had made his catch and brought it aboard in a canvas bag provided from the gunner's store. The cat hadn't liked it and had sworn, hissed and scratched all the way through the docks, making the bag sway and lift as though it was itself alive. The cat, by good fortune, happened to be a black one. Mr Cantley was delighted. He came down to the gunner's store to examine it.

He said, 'Well done, Stripey. Have much trouble, did you?'

'Not arf I didn't, sir!' Trudge was wet through with rain and sweat and his fat face was like a beetroot. There had been plenty of cats, as he'd expected, but they'd all been too fast for him until he'd nabbed this one like a sitting duck, flat out asleep in a coil of rope alongside a harbour tug. Having nabbed it, Stripey had moved fast out of range of the tug, to which the cat might well have belonged. That wasn't all. 'Nearly got done by the perishing police, sir. Copper saw me bag. When I opened it, the bloody cat almost got away again. Copper jumped a mile like he'd sat on a pin, sir.'

'But you talked your way out of it, eh?'

'Yessir,' Trudge said virtuously. 'Told a white lie, sir, said it was *our* bloody cat what had bug – what had jumped ship like, sir.'

Stripey, with the new acquisition confined until after sailing in the gunner's store, went down to the mess for his tot of rum; he felt he'd really earned it, bloody cat. When Hands to Dinner was piped over the tannoy, Stripey found time to write a letter, laboriously, to his missus in Bermondsey, where she lived with their married daughter: Stripey had an accommodating son-in-law who found Mum useful in the fish-and-chip business he ran. Stripey disliked him neverthe-less as he was mostly on the fiddle and had faked up some disease or disability that had made him unfit to be called up, bloody coward leaving it to an old Fleet Reservist like his father-in-law to fight for King and country and the bloody shop. Not good enough for Ethel, never had been . . . Stripey chewed the end of an indelible pencil and gazed for inspiration at some pin-ups on the mess bulkhead. Let a matloe be in a ship just one minute, Stripey thought, and he shoves up the nearest he can get to a bit of bare crumpet, not that Jane of the *Daily Mirror* was all that bare, but the others hadn't got much on and one had tits like barrage balloons. Inspiration came; chortling, Stripey penned some intimate details of the first thing he was going to do to the missus when he next got leave, mostly for the erudition of the officer who, before the ship sailed, would censor it. Officers needed to know a thing or two that they hadn't learned at their posh schools – the young ones, anyway. Officers didn't grow up as fast as the lower deck.

At 1500 hours the hands were piped to stations for leaving harbour and the Special Sea Dutymen and the cable and side party went to their positions fore and aft. At 1516 Archer reported to Cameron that the ship was ready to proceed. Cameron climbed to the forebridge; Burton was waiting with the Yeoman of Signals and the bridge lookouts and messenger. Below in the wheelhouse the coxswain was at the wheel, with a telegraphsman and a helmsman standing by. On the starting platform in the engine-room, Chief Engine-Room Artificer Osgood waited for the pointers on the telegraphs to move over. Osgood was a thin, nervy-looking man, hatchet-faced, hawk-eyed. Those eyes were everywhere. A nagger, was CERA Osgood, never satisfied – already his staff had found that out. Pacing like a panther, finding fault where none existed, always worried that some officer was going to come down on him like a ton of bricks for something left undone. According to Leading Stoker Morris, he needn't have worried his arse about that, since the *Palatine* didn't carry an engineer officer and the executive officers wouldn't know an overheating bearing from a girl's fanny. And, again according to Morris, that was a funny thing: a Chief ERA in full charge – a destroyer usually carried at least a warrant engineer. Osgood would need to be watch on, stop on, which must surely mean the engines weren't going to be wanted for any lengthy trip.

On the bridge Cameron passed the order fore and aft to single up and then right on time the remaining wires and ropes were let go. In the engine-room the telegraph pointers had already moved to Stand By Main Engines. As more bells rang, they moved again, this time to Slow Astern Both Engines. Here we go, Osgood thought, and prayed he wouldn't be let down by any cack-handed junior ratings. So far, he didn't know what they were like. Somewhere, someone had blundered in his view. Must be a rush job, and no other destroyers available . . . normally you expected some sort of working-up period to allow the hands to shake down, to make them into a team. Cameron had had similar thoughts and in fact had expressed them to NOIC, but Crooke had retorted crisply that the exigencies of the service meant that a commanding officer must accept unpromising situations and make the best of them. It wouldn't be the first time a new ship's company had faced action. That was true: the battleship *Prince of Wales* had barely commissioned when, together with the *Hood*, she had been brought to action in the Denmark Strait by the *Bismarck*.

Palatine moved off the wall. Cameron put his engines ahead and followed astern of *Panoply* and *Probity*, making across the dirty, rain-pocked water for the locks. He took up his binoculars: Barry Roads loomed. The Somerset shore lay invisible behind. The mist had cleared away now, but the visibility was far from good in the teeming rain, and there was a wind blowing strongly from westward. The convoy was on the move now, already dimly lit by shaded blue stern lights, the only lights permissible in wartime and essential for station-keeping. The lumbering merchant ships were being shepherded into some sort of order by armed trawlers and two more destroyers out of Cardiff that would remain with the convoy after *Palatine*, *Panoply* and *Probity* had broken off. The convoy was a large one, its columns stretching away past Sully Island and the army's ordnance depot to the east, past the tip of Barry Island to the west, an unwieldy collection of merchantmen of all shapes and sizes and speeds, a nightmare to the convoy commodore and the senior officer of the escort that would remain in company through the channel.

Palatine moved through the lock, out into Barry Roads. Cameron was under orders to take station astern of the centre column, while *Panoply* and *Probity* took up their positions on the port and starboard beams respectively.

'Half ahead both engines,' Cameron said. 'Wheel five degrees to port.'

Burton passed the order down to the coxswain at the wheel. King's response came back hollowly: 'Half ahead both engines, sir, wheel five degrees to port.' There was a pause. 'Five o' port wheel on, sir, engines repeated half ahead.'

'Midships . . . steady.'

'Steady, sir. Course, 145, sir.'

'Steer 140.' The first thing was to get to eastward of the convoy so as to come up astern.

'Steer 140, sir.' Another pause. 'Course 140, sir,' King said. This, he knew, would be a time of constant alterations until the destroyer was in her allotted station; alterations of speed as well, a handful of revolutions up and down as the ships of the convoy sorted themselves out and settled down in their steaming pattern. For King's money, that wouldn't be before they were off Lundy Island at the entrance to the Bristol Channel. King kept his mind on the job with a full alertness that years of experience had made second nature, an automatic response. That didn't mean he couldn't think other thoughts at the same time, and that was what he was doing. They weren't far off Somerset, where he'd been brought up before his family had moved to the Portsmouth area, thus making him, when he joined the service, a Pompey rating. King had a lot of memories of Somerset; he'd lived in Minehead, just across the water at this moment. That was where he'd first known Lizzie . . . a boyhood sweetheart who had become his wife and he'd never looked at anyone else. The walks they used to have along the shore, when he'd talked of going to sea . . . they came back vividly now as the

20

Palatine moved on through the darkening water. Oh, he'd gone to sea all right and he'd enjoyed his life even though too often it had meant long absences in the Med, or China, or Singapore. Each homecoming was another honeymoon that interspersed his climbing of the ladder from Seaman Boy Second Class to Chief Petty Officer, not of course that he'd been a bundle man – as the old Navy used to call the married men – when he was at the training establishment HMS *St Vincent* in Gosport, but he'd got hitched as a young AB. Never regretted it; never regretted the consequential lack of spending money abroad, the need to send every saved penny home to Lizzie in addition to the allotment note made out to Mrs Elizabeth King through the Paymaster Commander at RNB, which in fact had taken care of most of his pay. He only wished he was still paying it away; for a daft fleeting moment he wondered if Lizzie was there with him now, somewhere overhead, watching out for his safety on this job . . . he was so close to what had been home. If he got the chance, that Hitler was going to get a pasting. Lizzie had been visiting a sick aunt in Coventry on one of the nights in the winter of 1940–41 when the Jerry bombers had come over and he'd got the news on returning to Scapa after a North Atlantic convoy. If he'd been at home he'd never have let her go, sick aunt or not. After that, he'd spent his leaves with his parents, both now in their late seventies. Their cottage in Rowlands Castle near Pompey was now home to Tiny King's kids as well. They should be safe enough there. Four pubs and a handful of houses was no great target for any Luftwaffe. But soon enough now the boy would be following him into the Navy . . . King sent up a prayer that the war would be over before that happened.

The skipper's voice could be heard again, before Lieutenant Burton passed the order down for another alteration of course. King slid the wheel through his hands, made his standard responses back up the pipe. On the forebridge Cameron watched the dim blue of the stern lights, going over and over the operation in his mind, trying to foresee everything, dreaming up situations that hadn't been covered at the conference, extravagant situations unlikely enough to occur in fact, but in war you could never be complacent, never take anything for granted. He tried, not for the first time since reaching Barry, to take some stock of his officers and men. Archer should be all right: the basic RN training was there. All the same he had something of a dilettante air; for one thing he was a shade over-dressed for destroyers. He wore one of those long pointed stiff collars with a gap at the join where the knot of the tie went, so that the tie looked as though it grew out of the neck – they were called York collars, produced by Gieves, very elegant. The navigator, Burton, would be dependable. He had a solid, assured look and he'd been at sea for twenty-odd years. If he'd been a pre-war RNR rather than a wartime temporary he would have had commander's rank by now. And the others? *Palatine* carried two RNVR sub-lieutenants, Hope and Terry-Jones, in addition to a midshipman and Mr Cantley. Cantley's status as warrant gunner spoke for itself; and Midshipman Richards looked as if he had the makings despite his youth. But Hope and Terry-Jones had both come from battle-wagons and a different sort of war, and until 1940 when they'd been conscripted – neither had volunteered – as ordinary seamen, had been respectively a sales rep with a publishing firm and an architect. Without being in the least disparaging, Cameron was very aware that they had yet to show their paces as effective executive officers in a destroyer. Cameron felt that the bottoms of a few barrels had been scraped to get the *Palatine* away on her mission. And he didn't mean just the officers. There was not a lot of sea experience on the lower deck, apart from the backbone of the senior petty officers. . . .

'Coming up to Lundy, sir,' Burton said at 1930 hours.

'Thank you, Pilot. Yeoman?'

'Yessir?'

'Watch out for signals from the Commodore and *Panoply*.'

'Aye, aye, sir.' Yeoman of Signals Leckwith lifted his binoculars but sucked his teeth a little. He didn't need to be taught his job, certainly not by an RNVR. Leckwith had done six months as an instructor at HMS *King Alfred* in Hove in Sussex, helping, in the uninspiring ambience of what had been intended to be the municipal swimming-baths, to turn ordinary seamen into temporary sub-lieutenants RNVR. Because he had been consumed with disgusted envy at the apparent ease with which wartime ODs got promoted way over his head to commissions, he had proved so tetchy and scathing an instructor that he had been given a draft back to sea, which rankled, because Hove had been a nice, soft billet. Muttering to himself now, he watched out for the expected signals. The convoy and escorts would be ordered to make the turn to port south of Lundy to head down for the Wolf Rock, not an easy turn in the case of so unhandy and large a collection of ships. But when the signal came it was not the preparative for the turn.

Yeoman Leckwith's voice was loud and high. 'From the Commodore, sir, submarine attack starboard!'

3

Cameron snapped, 'Action stations!'

Burton pressed the alarm rattler button. The din cascaded through the ship. The watch below turned out in double-quick time, already dressed except for seaboots and duffel-coats hastily pulled on. Feet clattered on steel ladders as the guns' crews ran for the main and secondary armament. Cantley ran aft to the depth charges to see the pistols pushed home and the depth-charge party ready for orders from the forebridge. Petty Officer Todd, gunner's mate, went first to the fo'c'sle to pep up the crews of one and two guns. From the forebridge Cameron saw the signals passing between the Commodore and the escort leader. Swathes showed in the darkness, the wakes throwing up the sea as the vessels of the escort raced to starboard to start the attack. In response to orders from Captain Farnon in *Panoply*, Cameron ordered the wheel hard over to starboard and *Palatine*, heeling heavily to her rudder's action, crossed the stern of the convoy and then, under port helm, began moving fast up the flank.

'Asdics?' Cameron called out.

'No contact, sir,' a voice answered from the Asdic cabinet.

'Keep trying.'

'Aye, aye, sir.' The Asdic sounds came hollowly, ghostlike. Wind tore across the destroyer's decks and the confused sea threw solid water aboard throughout her length. For a while time seemed in suspense, with nothing happening. Then very suddenly the night was lit by an appalling explosion on the starboard side of the convoy's van, followed closely by

24

another. Debris was flung into the air, some of it clearly human. A blast of heat swept back momentarily. Burton said, 'Ammunition ships most likely. *Forest Hill* and *Jonathan Norton* . . . they both had a full cargo from the ordnance depot at Sully. Poor bastards!'

'And bloody bad luck,' Cameron said savagely. Two ammunition ships together – it was almost as though they had been picked out by the U-boat's captain. As he conned his ship on, still waiting for a positive report from the Asdics, another ship went, this time not so spectacularly. There was a dull booming sound followed by a subdued reddish glow. The convoy plodded on, brave but lethal in its own right – the station-keeping was by now all over the show, though no order had come from the Commodore to scatter. Away to his port side there came the sad din of tearing metal as two of the ships collided. Cameron cursed. Virtually only just out of the Bristol Channel and five ships were sunk or damaged. Such was the toll of the war at sea, a war in which Britain couldn't afford the terrible and long-sustained losses of valuable ships and experienced seamen. He had passed the order to stand by depth charges when the Asdic reported a contact.

'Dead ahead, sir, one thousand yards.'

'Hold it.' The note had changed now, was higher, faster. *Palatine* went on under full power. In the engine-room Chief ERA Osgood fingered his chin and snapped at everyone in sight. In a voice not quite low enough despite the engine-room noise, ERA Hoskin said dispassionately, 'Daft old bastard, why don't you go and get stuffed.'

Osgood gaped. 'What was that, Hoskin?'

'Nothing, Chief.'

'Yes it was, I heard it. Any more o' that, my lad, and you'll be in Jimmy's report, all right?'

Hoskin, alongside Osgood on the starting platform, shrugged. Nothing wrong with the old bugger's hearing if he could pick up a *sotto voce* remark in the din of an engine-room . . . not for the first time in the last twenty-four hours Hoskin reckoned the Chief had taught himself to lip-read nasty comments on himself – either that or he used telepathy. In the middle of the run-up to action, it all grated on Hoskin. Maybe the Chief didn't know there was a war on. A moment later the whole engine-room rang and thumped to the racket of exploding depth charges – not far off, much too bloody close, they could spring some rivets if the skipper didn't watch it. They could start to flood. Well, if they did, they might at least be out of that special mission and that was something – by this time, everyone aboard knew they weren't going all the way with the convoy. You didn't embark marines for escort duty, not unless you were a capital ship that carried bootnecks as a matter of course and bullshit.

Up in the fresh air denied the engine-room and stokehold complements, Cameron had seen the signal from the escort leader: '*Attacking.*' As the leader thundered on past the point of drop of her depth charges, *Probity* was seen to be racing in across her wake. Another pattern rose, took the sea and went deep. More spouts of water, seen in the continuing blaze from the dying arms carriers. Impossible to see whether or not there was any oil coming to the surface, but Cameron was watching closely through his binoculars. Then star-shell broke ahead, bringing up the whole scene as the blobs of brilliant light drifted downward, and Cameron called to Burton.

'U-boat on the surface, Pilot.' He shouted down over the bridge screen to Sub-Lieutenant Hope, Officer of the Quarters on the for'ard guns. 'Surfaced, Hope. Fine on the starboard bow. Stand by to open.'

'Aye, aye, sir,' Hope called back breathlessly. This, as it happened, was the first time he'd seen action, seen violent destruction and bodies hurled into the air like chaff before the wind, and it had shaken him badly. It was different from anything he'd ever known. Booksellers might not always be pleased to see you when they were busy, but they didn't blow you up. Peter Hope hadn't known any enmity in his young life and now the whole of Hitler's war machine was out to get him. The horror of it was beyond any of his imaginings, but he took a grip and waited for the next order from the Captain. It soon came, but it was an anti-climax. Cameron called again from the bridge, just after the harsh crack of gunfire had come from ahead.

'We won't waste ammo,' Cameron said. 'She's going down by the stern already.'

'Very good, sir. Are we going to pick up survivors, sir?'

'Don't be an idiot, Hope.'

Hope flushed beneath his anti-flash gear. 'Sorry, sir.' He supposed it was idiotic; there could be other U-boats around and you didn't risk British ships to rescue Jerries and he tried to tell himself he didn't care anyway. It was them or him and his shipmates and Jerries were Jerries, full stop. But he thought about them, twisting and turning as they went down to the bottom of the sea, then in due course came up again, and floated, and gradually filled with air as the flesh rotted, and became like balloons of stinking gas. The thought made him retch horribly, as was noticed by Leading Seaman Cusson, captain of number one gun. Poor little bugger, Cusson thought, he'll get used to it, given time. Maybe. Some never did. Depended on how tough you were mentally. Or how resistant to the idea of sudden death. How much of a bastard, perhaps, since you couldn't call war anything but revolting and if it didn't touch your mind you had, by any civilized standards, to be a bastard. Leading Seaman Cusson had had a hard war to date, sunk three times already, and he'd seen plenty of his mates die, either drowned or blown to pieces by the Jerry guns, or screaming blue murder with burns that you'd have thought would have killed them instantly. Perhaps he was a bastard himself now because he'd got past turning a hair, got past thinking about it. He grinned at Sub-Lieutenant Hope and said, 'All in the day's work, sir. If someone's going to win, someone else has to go like. And me, I'd rather it was the Jerries, wouldn't you?'

Hope nodded. 'Yes. Yes, of course.'

'Cheer up, then, sir. More we finish off, sooner it'll all be over.'

'I was thinking of the men in the convoy.'

Cusson grunted non-committally. He was bloody certain young Hope had been thinking of the Jerries, left behind when they could have been picked up – he'd only just asked the question of the skipper. Cusson thought that was soft, no way to pursue a war. You had to be single-minded . . . becoming a bastard again? He dismissed it from his mind and thought instead about his hammock below in the messdeck. Back to kip would suit him nicely, and he had a couple of bars of nutty in his locker, made his mouth water just to think about them. But unknown to Cusson, orders were coming through from *Panoply* by shaded Aldis lamp. Yeoman Leckwith reported to Cameron, having read.

'From Senior Officer, sir. *Await executive.*'

Burton looked puzzled. 'Meaning what?' he asked.

'Previous orders,' Cameron answered. 'A little before I expected, Pilot. The U-boat attack seems to have precipitated something.'

Burton said, 'Don't you think it's time I was told the orders? Not that I haven't made some guesses,' he added.

'Any moment now, Pilot. As to the guesses – yes, it's not been too difficult. The marines were a dead give-away.' Cameron paused. 'Talking of the marines, send down word that I'd like the Major to come up.'

Burton passed the order to the bridge messenger. Within the next half-minute the executive signal was made and reported by the yeoman. *Panoply* swung away from the convoy, moving fast under full power, followed by *Probity* and *Palatine*. Cameron gave Burton a course for the Bishop Rock off the Scillies.

'And after that, sir?'

Cameron gave a tight grin. 'Brest,' he said. 'Sorry about the sealed lips, Pilot. Shades of Stanley Baldwin . . . I was under strict orders.'

Burton had already turned for his chart table in rear of the forebridge. He had it all worked out. 'A little under 240 miles,' he said. 'Say seven hours steaming at our present speed . . . ETA off Brest, 0230 hours. How's that, sir?'

'Gives us an hour in hand, Pilot. The landing's timed for 0330, which is when the tide's just right. Do you know Brest?'

Burton said, 'I've been in there, yes, before I joined P & O. And I've been looking at the chart, having made those guesses. What do we do – go alongside, and land the commandos, is that it?'

Cameron nodded.

'Going to remain closed up at action stations?'

'Yes, all the way through.' Cameron turned as the First Lieutenant came up to the forebridge accompanied by the Major of Marines. He repeated what he'd said to Burton, that the ship would remain at full readiness, apart from short stand-downs for a few hands at a time. After a word with Major Shawcross, Cameron told Archer that he was going to speak to the ship's company, using the loud hailer directed fore and aft once they were clear of the convoy. He would speak to the Chief ERA by means of the voice-pipe and leave it to him to inform the engine-room complement.

What he had to say when they were clear was brief enough: under the overall command of Captain Farnon in *Panoply*, the destroyer force would enter the port of Brest under cover of darkness, moving at full speed and wearing no colours. Once through the Goulet de Brest and past La Cormorandière beacon on the north-eastern tip of the Presqu'île de Quélern, the ships would enter between the breakwaters and go alongside the wall in the inner harbour. As they came alongside the battle ensigns would be broken out and the commandos would land immediately. 'The objective,' Cameron said, 'will be the bomb-proof U-boat shelters which air recce missions have shown to be under construction behind caissons in the main harbour, inside the breakwater.' He paused. 'You may ask, why not send in the RAF to bomb them out of existence before they're ready. The answer is, the Foreign Office doesn't want to see heavy casualties among the French civilians. So the commandos are going in with demolition charges to attack and destroy the shelters direct.

29

Of course, as we all know, there has been heavy bombing in the past, notably when the German heavy ships were in the port – *Scharnhorst, Gneisenau, Prinz Eugen.* A good deal of damage was done to the port installations during those raids, but not much to the ships. There were French casualties . . . and there's not to be any more if humanly possible. But we have to knock out the Jerries' U-boat bases, of which Brest is a main one. Don't forget, they can send U-boats out from Brest to points beyond the range of our own air and sea escorts, and all the convoys are at risk.'

That was all he had to say. It was enough. The ship seethed with comment. As the gunner's mate remarked to the buffer, why all the sanctimonious cossetting of the French? 'Bloody Frogs, most of the buggers are Vichy!'

Bartlett disagreed. 'Not all, they're not. How about the Resistance, then, eh? Likely enough they'll be in on this with us.'

'Yes, well.'

'Yes well what?'

'Oh, bollocks to 'em,' Todd said, and added scathingly, 'Why is it the Andrew has always to pull the bloody Brylcreem Boys' chestnuts out of the fire for 'em, tell me that if you can!'

There was a lot of similar comment elsewhere on deck and below. Nobody in the other two services had too much time for the RAF; the RAF was never there when it was wanted – so ran the unfair story; the fact that the admirals and generals always did what they could to inhibit the air marshals was disregarded or simply not advertised. Inter-service rivalry was not by any means absent in wartime. The RAF was an infant still and must not be encouraged towards precocity . . . and it was always handy and satisfactory to have a whipping-boy. Chief ERA Osgood liked whipping-boys and as he stared around his engine-room all set for nit-picking his mind roved over past RAF iniquities – the British ships they had sunk and the British troops they had bombed or shot up just because they were half barmy and couldn't see straight or

30

read maps or whatever it was they did read in the air. All because of them and some daft ha'porth in Whitehall who didn't want dead Frogs, he was here now, hurtling towards God knew what. Not that he would ever shirk anything in the way of duty, it was just that he considered it all bloody unnecessary. Aircraft could do a better job. There was another point: Osgood couldn't see it coming off. The Jerries would spot them miles off. They would steam straight into hell.

Archer, going about his duties as First Lieutenant, seeing to the effectiveness of the damage control parties and fire parties, making sure all was secure along the upper deck as the *Palatine* sent her bow wave swathing back along her sides, organizing a scratch meal from the galley to be sent to the hands at their action stations, also felt doubts. More so than Osgood: this, Archer believed, was to be a hundred per cent suicide mission; he had seen the detailed orders and plans by now. The destruction of the bomb-proof submarine pens was considered vital. This came from a very high level: there was more than a whiff of large, expensive cigars. Every man would do his duty – that was more like Nelson. No hanging back, just get there and lay the charges and make sure they went off.

Not much was said about how they got back to the UK afterwards, those that were still alive. The Major was making the bland assumption that *Panoply*, *Probity* and *Palatine* would still be there waiting. Well, maybe they would be, but only maybe, Archer thought. The Germans wouldn't be hanging around doing damn all. Brest had been one of the French Navy's principal bases and was strongly defended by the Germans, had been ever since the fall of France. If only they were to have air cover . . . but of course that was the whole point of using the Navy. No use moaning. Archer caught himself up sharp. He mustn't look despondent. Never let it be said of him that he spread alarm amongst the hands by wearing a long face or looking as sick as he felt. He and the gunner were the only RN officers, the only straight-stripers, in

31

the ship. The only ones who'd been trained explicity for war. They had to be the ramrods.

But no one was looking happy about it all, except the RM commandos, who obviously had the blood-lust and were itching to go. Petty Officer Stibbs, fo'c'sle divisional PO, saw that plainly in their faces as he moved through the crowded messdecks. The commandos wouldn't appear in the open until the last moment, except for a handful currently puking their guts up on deck, hanging over the guardrails to loo'ard. Along the messdecks they sat or stood clutching their rifles and a lot more besides. Talk about an armoury.

'Everything but the kitchen sink, son,' Stibbs said to a lance-corporal. 'FN automatic rifles, bayonets, stens, mortars, grenades . . . not to mention all the bloody demolition stuff.' He looked the youthful NCO full in the face. 'Can't wait, eh?'

'That's right, PO.' The lad, Stibbs thought, was bung full of confidence.

'Done it before, have you?'

'Only on exercises. Wales and Scotland.'

'Tough?'

The lance-corporal grinned. 'Ever been in the Brecon Beacons, or around Glencoe?'

'Never,' Stibbs said, glad enough to be able to say it. At least you could get warm on board a ship, and dry too sometimes. But he had an idea the commandos would find reality rather different from exercises. Exercises were all very well and they made them realistic enough, but at heart you knew you weren't in mortal danger, that the bullets that sang over your head were not aimed at you direct. In just a few hours' time, they would be. Stibbs expected a murderous fire to meet them the moment they entered if not before. But the commandos didn't seem worried; they checked their weapons time and again, they drank cocoa from the big urn in the galley, they whistled and sang. No whistling aboard a ship, but Stibbs hadn't the heart to stop them even though, being Royal Marines and not ordinary pongoes, they ought to have known for themselves. But the marines had become a different sort of outfit by this stage of the war; most of them were more soldier than sailor, most of them were in fact commando-trained rather than doused in the bullshit side of blues and pipe-clayed helmets. They had a colour-sergeant to match, too: a granite-faced giant named Mather who looked as though he was just out of Dartmoor after a spell for manslaughter. Colour-Sergeant Mather was housed in the petty officers' mess and Stibbs had had a word with him before they'd cleared away from Barry docks. It was difficult since Mather didn't say much beyond 'Aye' or 'No' in a disinterested voice but in the end he'd unbent enough to say that in pre-war days he'd been a boxer doing the booths at fairs and such and after having joined the Fourth Dragoons at the outbreak of war he'd been transferred to the Royal Marines for commando training duties – he'd broken too many recruits to the dragoons after being made an NCO, and the Colonel had felt he was a deterrent to new entries.

'And I bet you've broken more since,' Stibbs said.

'Aye, I have that.' Mather clammed up again after that, possibly in case he was questioned as to his current mission. Well, Stibbs thought now as he moved on through the mess-deck, they knew by this time. He looked at his watch: three hours to go before the world blew up around them. Stibbs, who had done what no one was supposed to do – bottled his tot – made his way to the POs' mess to pour the contents of the bottle, only two days' issues, down his throat. He felt a bit better after that. He went back on deck, the wind tearing at his oilskin and duffel-coat, the latter on top. Perishing cold, you needed all you could drag on. The sea was getting up and that could operate in their favour if it held to the French coast, which it probably would. Brest was washed by the northern part of the Bay of Biscay where it seemed always to be blowing in his experience, and some bad weather just might help to obscure their approach. The Jerries might not be at their most alert, for one thing. And there wouldn't be any moon for another. The sky was beautifully overcast. Keeping

33

a close watch all round from the forebridge, Cameron appreciated the point as well, though it was not unexpected: the weathermen had confirmed it all in advance, and indeed the operation had been planned around the Met forecasts. The ships could steal in quite a way before they were spotted. Or dash rather than steal. This thing had to be bold, Farnon had said at the Barry conference, and the speed would be maintained until the last possible moment. It would be a difficult manoeuvre for all three ships: from full ahead to full astern at precisely the right instant to bring the vessels up all standing alongside. Easy to make a cock-up and hit the wall.

He said as much to the Major, who had remained on the bridge with him. Shawcross said, 'You'll be all right.'

'We hope!'

'Better be, old man. We're all dependent on you in the first instance.'

There was the rub. Cameron turned away and paced the small space between the binnacle and fore rail. Command was a two-edged sword. You had to be right all the time, no room for mistakes and misjudgments. You got the kudos and you got the blame, and if the blame was justified then you never forgave yourself. If lives were involved, you'd live with it for the rest of your days. There was no relaxation for a captain at sea. Watch on, stop on, and keep alert however bloody tired you were, however cold and hungry, however worried. And at the same time look confident. Guns' crews, depth-charges parties, helmsmen, lookouts, they could all be accorded relieve-decks facilities for short periods even at action stations when nothing was currently happening. But not the Captain.

As he passed him for the tenth time, Shawcross said, 'D'you know, I think you and your people have got the worst end of the stick in this.'

Cameron grinned. 'Don't be modest, Major!'

'No, I mean it. We'll be in there . . . being active. Not you. You've got the waiting job. The nail-biting one. Not that you're going to be left unmolested, of course,' he added

34

lightly.

'You can say that again. But we'll be there when you come back.'

Shawcross clapped him on the shoulder but said nothing further. Shawcross was a regular officer and as tough as his colour-sergeant basically, though it didn't show in quite the same way. Cameron had gleaned that he was a widower with four children, ages ranging from one to ten. His wife had died in childbirth. Cameron couldn't help thinking about the motherless children. The chances were they would soon be fatherless as well. Any man who led a mission of this sort would be damned lucky to come through and Shawcross must know that. The kids . . . one day it would be a source of pride, but before that day came and things had receded into the background of their young lives there was going to be a terrible vacuum.

Cameron looked at the clock, the face dimly lit below the other instruments and dials in front of him. Just over an hour to go. Below, Cantley would now be issuing rifles and ammunition to the ship's company, for what use that would be if it came to close-quarter fighting.

4

At one stage of the war, after Hitler had ordained Brest a fortress, there had been something like a whole division based on the port: but by this time many of the troops had been withdrawn to other theatres. In the war's earlier days Brest had been a centre of a fair amount of action. Back in June 1940 a series of demolitions had been carried out in the port by the French assisted by a British party, and of course since then there had been the long-continued bombings by Coastal Command and Bomber Command; and Coastal Command had carried out some largely ineffective mining operations in the Brest approaches, as had the Navy's minelayers. But latterly, and especially since the German heavy ships had been withdrawn, things had quietened a good deal for the garrison and a degree of relaxation had crept in; the alertness was not quite what it had been. And the garrison knew that if ever the British attacked again, it would be in the form of more bombings – they wouldn't come by sea. The British were stupid but not entirely insane. And like all bombings, it would be more a case of sound than fury unless it was conducted at saturation level along the lines of the splendid Luftwaffe's attacks on London and Coventry, Portsmouth, Bristol, Plymouth, Liverpool . . . and the British, they hadn't the strength for that. They were undoubtedly going to lose the war. Herr Hitler, glorious Chancellor of the glorious Third Reich, was in the ascendant still and would rise even higher. Of course, there had been some setbacks, notably to Rommel's Afrika Corps, and via the greasy

Italians who always ran away, never having recovered from Caporetto in the last war, but all that was only to be expected. No nation could win all the time, and the Führer would most certainly be in good heart.

Such sentiments were running through the mind of Hauptmann Hans-Dietrich von Arendt, himself late of the glorious Afrika Corps, as he stared into the sky from the coastal radar station of which he had the honour to be in command. He strode up and down the open space surrounding the radar buildings, just as if on parade in barracks, deeply breathing the air that was now German. Von Arendt believed strongly in physical fitness . . . but watched the overcast skies at the same time, being a conscientious soldier of the Reich. Overcast, yes – no, the British would not come! Not tonight, probably never. The rubbish was on the run. There had been talk of a Second Front one of these fine days, talk of the Führer moving no less than twenty-eight divisions of his army because of it, moving them to the coast between Brest and Den Helder in the north, land of the deplorable Dutchmen who considered themselves as good as Germans. But there was so far no sign of any Second Front and also, in and around Brest, no sign of any of the twenty-eight divisions. Time would tell, but Hans-Dietrich von Arendt didn't believe a word of it as he strode, breathed, and watched. The Führer would not allow himself to be panicked, and there were still the Russians to be watched and fought, filthy communists who were very much more of a menace than the effete and half-beaten British. Von Arendt, who had scuttled out of North Africa via Cape Bon a little ahead of Field Marshal Rommel, didn't regard the British Eighth Army as having been victorious nor himself defeated. Oh, no. The so brave Afrika Corps . . . Rommel, known as the Fox for his wiliness, had fooled the British by a splendid tactical withdrawal. What use was North Africa in any case? Arabs and other bandits abounded, dirty, non-Aryan people; though it was said that the Führer had been extremely angry, going indeed into one of his famous rages.

Here in Brest there would be no need for the Führer to be upset. Von Arendt continued looking up at the lowering sky. Poor flying weather indeed, very poor. And there was nothing on the radar screen.

Then something happened. Something untoward and very fast. Von Arendt, turning to go back into the building, became aware of a flitting form, darkly clad, in the night's gloom. Something came down over his head, a smelly sack, and he felt his arms pinioned. Struggle was useless. The *verdamt* Resistance! Another pair of arms went round his face and the sack – it had been a manure sack – was pressed into his mouth like a gag. Then he was lifted bodily and carried away.

Out at sea, now beginning the approach to the Chenal du Toulinguet from south-westerly, Cameron had the German coastal radar much in mind. Farnon had spoken of certain arrangements made; but the men and women of the *maquis* were not infallible. On the other hand the conditions were not favourable for radar; the sea was running high, with sizeable waves, and the destroyers were low in the water, hard to pick up in the prevailing weather.

'What d'you think?' he asked the navigator.

Burton shrugged. 'I'm not too worried, sir. Not yet. When we're closer in . . .'

He didn't finish the sentence but Cameron got the drift. Closer in, the water would flatten. But by then it probably wouldn't matter. It couldn't be long before they were seen visually, never mind the radar. Cameron was tense now; there was tension throughout the ship, all hands alert to their finger-tips and busy with speculation of a nightmare kind. Even the commandos, now with their exposed flesh blackened, were silent by this time. Taut nerves were indicated by the hard grip on the weapons along the electrically-lit messdecks, in the grimness of the marines' expressions as they listened to every sound from the upper deck. Cameron had kept them informed as to distance from time to time, distance and the prevailing weather conditions, sending Sub-Lieutenant Terry-Jones down to speak to them. When Terry-Jones appeared on the messdeck they were not impressed, making the assumption that he was the only officer the skipper felt like sparing from his place of duty – Terry-Jones was somewhat baby-faced and there would have been some polite leg-pulling if it hadn't been for Colour-Sergeant Mather. Mather stalked along behind him with his pace-stick under his arm – you could never part the colour-sergeant from that bloody article, it seemed – and whenever addressed by Terry-Jones slammed his boots into the deck and screamed out 'Sir!' which activity caused plenty of whispered comment and grins from such of the Naval ratings as had been temporarily stood down from their stations. The Navy wasn't so demonstrative, not unless you happened to be the chief gunner's mate of the parade at Whaley when you almost drowned in bull.

Stripey Trudge was more concerned about the shanghaied cat than about anything else. Poor little sod, it didn't seem happy and he, Stripey, was the immediate cause of its discomfiture as it fled from before the colour-sergeant and spat vituperatively from the empty hammock netting – all the hammocks had been nicked by the First Lieutenant for placing around the forebridge and the multiple pom-pom position and other exposed places as some protection against blast, splinters and bullets. The cat, which had been named, naturally enough, Barry, glittered its eyes and looked trapped and angry. Maybe it wasn't a seagoing cat after all, Stripey thought, just a harbour tug one, as he'd suspected on capture. Maybe it missed its dock-scavenging mates. Or maybe, being a cat, it had had a premonition.

Stripey shivered suddenly.

Premonitions. His old dad had believed in them, his old dad who'd bought it at Jutland, blown to kingdom come by a shell that had landed on his gun-turret aboard one of Admiral Beatty's battle-cruisers. Accounts afterwards said that turret had gone red hot. His poor old dad had bloody fried like an

39

egg. And talk about premonitions: his dad had had lots of them in his time and every one had turned out right. He'd had one just before he was drafted to the old *Good Hope*, lost at Coronel with Sir Christopher Cradock – he'd got out of the draft by getting pissed and falling off the gangway when returning from shore; broke his leg, had Stripey's dad. He'd had another premonition before that – he was going to lose his rate of leading seaman. That was right and all . . . booze again. Another that he was going to have to swim for it when he joined the *Aboukir*. That hit the target too. The final one had come when he got that draft chit to join Beatty in the *Lion*: he'd had a dream in which he was burned to death . . .

'Bloody hell,' Stripey said aloud, eyes as lit-up as the cat's.

'Now what's up?' This was Leading Seaman Wicks, another three-badgeman with a gut to rival Trudge's.

'Premonitions,' Stripey said, sounding hollow and doomful.

'Oh, fer Gawd's sake . . . that's all we want, bloody premonitions!'

'You don't know the half of it,' Stripey said in an aggrieved tone.

'No, an' I don't want to, not till after we get back any road.'

'But look – '

'Shut up, Stripey.' Wicks turned away and lumbered off, making for the heads, which was what he'd come below for – have a pee. He'd just reached them when the bosun's mate began piping through the messdeck, recalling the stood-down men to their stations. The tension increased as there was a rush for the door into the galley flat and the upper deck. Any moment now . . . Stripey Trudge felt highly uneasy. Not himself a premonition man, just thinking about his old dad had actually given him one at last. God's vengeance for nicking a cat from safety?

On the forebridge Cameron's nails were digging into his palms. He was as yet unable to see the French coast and all was quiet: they hadn't been noticed but very soon they would be. After that, they would steam into something like the

40

reception accorded the Light Brigade at Balaclava. *Stormed at with shot and shell . . .*

The commando major said, 'I'll get below, Captain.'

'Your lads are all set?'

'Yes.'

'Well – you know the orders, Major. The moment we touch – '

'We go. And run like bloody hell!'

Cameron held out his hand. 'The best of luck to you all.'

'Thanks. You too.'

Shawcross sketched a formal salute and turned away down the ladder to the upper deck. Cameron listened to the clatter of his boots, wondering if he would hear them coming up again when all this was over. Up the ladder came the First Lieutenant. He reported, 'All hands closed up, sir. All watertight doors and hatches shut, ship ready to go alongside.'

'Thank you, Number One. Ready to go alongside . . . you make it sound like peacetime!'

Archer grinned. 'Well, in a sense the routine's the same. Except that it won't be quite like the Med Fleet entering Malta. Boats lowered, anchors let go, quarter and lower booms swung out . . . all that jazz . . . all together on the executive from the Flag.'

'Not quite,' Cameron said drily. 'This time it'll be even more spectacular, if more ragged.'

Archer nodded, felt the fear in the pit of his stomach, like a gnawing rodent. The orders were precise and at that moment Mr Cantley and the gunner's mate were making their separate rounds of the main and secondary armament ensuring that no man was in any doubt as to what those orders were.

'You, Spragg.' Petty Officer Todd stood square before a nineteen-year-old ordinary seaman, one of the hostilities-only variety, whose action station was on Number Three gun aft. 'Know what we're going to do, don't you?'

'Yes, PO.'

'Yes, PO,' Todd repeated in a flat voice. 'First thing you

should have bloody learned under training at *Royal Arthur*, you address a gunner's mate as GI – GI for gunnery instructor, right?'

Spragg said nervously. 'Sorry, GI. I forgot.'

'Forgot. In the 'eat of approaching action. Don't you go and forget anything else this night, Spragg, my lad. The orders are, we go in like bloody Guy Fawkes night. All right? The moment anyone's seen on shore in Nazi uniform, we go in with all guns blazing away at the bugger and any other buggers in his neighbourhood. Likewise *Panoply* and *Probity*. 'Is Majesty's coronation celebrations won't hold a bleedin' candle to it, right? So you lot,' he added, addressing his remarks generally now, 'you all keep your eyes open, report anything in case it's not been seen from the forebridge. Anyone that's blind, fall out now.'

It was a joke; so, to some extent, was the gunner's mate's ferocity of expression and most of them knew it. It went a little way towards relieving the tension and anxiety. Spragg gave a nervous giggle at the mention of anyone being blind. Todd scowled and said, 'That's right, laugh! I'm a funny man. Split me own sides at me own wit, I do.' Then he reached out and laid a hand on Spragg's shoulder. 'All right, lad. You'll do. Even if you shit yourself, an' that's no disgrace. First time's always bad – *action*, I refer to.'

He turned away and moved on aft. He encountered the gunner. He said, 'I'm bloody sorry for the poor sods. Dragged away from home and mum and pitched into this lot.' He rose and fell on the balls of his feet, hands behind his back, like a copper resting in a shop doorway.

'So were you and me in the first place,' Cantley said.

'Ah! But we had a career in mind, wanted to join. Half of these didn't, sir.'

The gunner poked a hard fist into Todd's stomach. 'Don't go soft on me, Jack.'

'Soft me arse. Just plain sympathy.'

'Just as bad. But I know what you mean. But remember this: don't let 'em see it. You and me, we're the drivers.'

Cantley paused. 'I'm not too happy about the wavy subs –
Hope and whosit – Terry-Jones. Still wet behind the ears. I
don't say they haven't got guts and I won't say it till I know
different, but I don't reckon they're going to stiffen anybody.
Except the cat. Leadership . . . it takes time to learn.'

Todd nodded. 'Talking of the cat, sir. *Your* cat, if I may be
so bold.'

'What about it?'

Todd said, 'Crapped in the hammock netting, just before
the watertight doors were clipped down. Buffer's doing 'is
nut.'

'Ha! What else is he doing?'

'Kicking the cat up the arse I shouldn't wonder.'

Cantley snorted and moved away, casting an eye over the
racks and throwers, though he had no anticipation of using
depth charges – yet you never could tell. Might come in handy
– the throwers, not the racks, of course. Bloody daft to drop
charges right beneath your own bum. He looked at the sea:
still high but, he thought, tending to lessen now as they came
into the lee of the land. Not so much wetness coming over. He
walked for'ard, passing beneath Number Three gun on the
after gun deck with the splinter shield over the entry to the
wardroom flat. Spragg looked down on him, enviously. A
gunner RN would be in his element, war was his forte, what
he'd trained for all his life. A gunner couldn't ever be afraid,
presumably, it wouldn't make sense. As for Spragg, he was
closer to what the gunner's mate had suggested than the
gunner's mate knew. He could feel an alarming wateriness
and he tried to shut his mind to that and to what lay so close
ahead. He thought of home, of his parents, of his young
brother and sister, all of them safe – he hoped – in Petersfield
in Hampshire. Small-town life suited his family and suited
him too; he couldn't wait for the war to end, had hated being
propelled into uniform and sent far away to the training
establishment *Royal Arthur* in Skegness. Marching, knots
and splices, more marching, boat-handling in what had been
the kids' lake – *Royal Arthur* had been a Butlin's holiday

camp before the war – and more marching. Screeching petty officers, and portly and toffee-nosed commanders apparently by the dozen . . . he hadn't liked any of it. He thought about the office where he'd worked before the war: he'd been dead lucky to be taken on as a clerk by a firm of estate agents with a branch office in Havant, just down the line. There had been a girl in the Havant office and Spragg had used every endeavour to get sent over on business, just to see her. She'd been about to become his girlfriend, he believed, when the call-up came. The Navy had wrecked that; when he went home on his first leave, she'd taken up with another bloke, very handy in the Havant office. It hadn't done much for his self-esteem – or his confidence.

Below him, the gunner passed on, trailing clouds of Naval glory. How any sane person could stay in the Andrew long enough to advance from seaman boy second class to the rank of warrant officer was quite beyond Spragg's comprehension. His thoughts shifted again as Leading Seaman Wicks, captain of Three gun, dropped something heavy on the deck of the gun platform and said, 'Beg pardon, doctor,' in a mincing voice. Spragg knew why: the wardroom, right below him, would have been turned into a medical dressing station all ready for action. Wicks went on, 'Bloody bang'll have made the quack fall arse over bollocks into his own po, shouldn't wonder, eh.'

It hadn't been quite so drastic, though Surgeon Lieutenant Pratt, RNVR, Pratt by name and Pratt by nature his fellow students at his medical school used to say, had started violently and broken out into a cold sweat. The bridge had already reported that they were now closing the French coast; this wasn't the time for sudden bangs; steel decks made nasty noises beneath when dropped on. Pratt's Leading Sick Berth Attendant noticed the quack's reaction and reassured him.

'Just some clumsy oaf up top, sir. Not to worry.'

'I'm not worried, Cleek.'

'Course not, sir.' Just shit-scared, LSBA Cleek reflected silently without surprise or criticism. He was scared himself

44

but he wouldn't admit it. 'Just think of Nelson, sir.'

'Nelson?' Dr Pratt stared myopically and his adam's-apple moved up and down in his long neck.

'That's right, sir. Nelson. Famous British admiral. Battle of Trafalgar, 18—'

'Yes, yes, I know all that, Cleek,' Pratt said testily. He resented the LSBA's remark. Nelson was synonymous with courage, and there had seemed to be some reason . . . Pratt breathed hard down his nose, lips set, and walked restlessly up and down in a stench of antiseptic, wondering what the medical dressing station was going to look like soon. He visualized a mass of blood, detached limbs, gutted stomachs, smashed heads and incipient gangrene. He might have to operate, cut off an arm or leg, remove lead from interiors. Dr Pratt had recently qualified MB, BS and was thus a kind of surgeon, but the only surgery he had done while in a hospital appointment had been routine stuff with an appendicectomy as his apex. He had lanced boils and sewn up cuts. Battle casualties were going to be different and he sweated again. If only there was a more senior doctor to whom he might turn if necessary. But that was wishing for the moon. All the armed forces were desperately short of doctors and vessels of *Palatine*'s size simply couldn't be spared more than one apiece, not even for a special mission. Back at the Royal Naval Hospital, Haslar, the drafted Pratt had asked the Surgeon Captain for advice. It had been crisp: 'Keep 'em alive if you can, then send 'em to the nearest hospital when you get back.'

The sound-powered telephone rang and Cleek answered it. 'Medical dressing station . . . yes, sir. Right-o, sir.' He hung the handset back on its hook and addressed Pratt. 'Forebridge again, sir. Starting the final run-in and not far to go.'

'Thank you, Cleek.'

Pratt paced the wardroom looking a prey to his nerves, very restless, checking over his medical arrangements for the umpteenth time. Then, as Cleek watched, he moved over to a miniature dispensary contained in a white-painted metal box

45

with a red cross on it. He drew out a bottle. Cleek couldn't see the label but he knew what it was: Dr J. Collis Browne's Chlorodyne, an excellent specific against diarrhoea. An old-fashioned remedy but still effective. Cleek, who was an active service rating, had seen it used before by an RN medical officer: a certain surgeon lieutenant-commander, steeped in gin and out of practice, who, but for Dr J. Collis Browne, would have remained glued to a seat in the heads when faced with the need to take out an appendix at sea. Well, it took all sorts . . . and most of them were in fact pretty good.

Pratt took his dose and started pacing again. Up and down, face twitching. The waiting was agony. It ended very suddenly when with no warning the thunder of the guns broke out overhead.

5

The decision had been made at the conference in Barry to make the south-westerly approach through the Chenal du Toulinguet on the grounds that the Germans might be less initially suspicious of any vessel entering by that route – it wasn't much but it was something – it might give them a few minutes. And it was a case of every little helps. Cameron had conned the ship in, astern of the leader and *Probity*. The speed of the force was being maintained: in unskilled hands it would have been, in a pilotage sense, suicide. Burton sweated blood; so did Cameron. It would have been bad enough in broad daylight, in normal times only a lunatic would enter at such speed. At night it was a thousand times worse. Rocks abounded: La Louve tower to eastward, marking a cluster of rocks off Toulinguet point, to the west the forty-foot high Le Pohen. To hold the middle of the fairway was vital, and there were no lights to guide them.

'Le Petit Minou ahead,' Burton warned. 'At least – I think so. This is where we stand by to bear to starboard, sir.'

Cameron, hands gripping the rail of the bridge screen, nodded. He could feel and hear the drum of his blood, the rapid beat of his heart. Steering towards Le Petit Minou on the north side of the Goulet de Brest, he passed the order to bear away to starboard for the passage of the Goulet itself. Now the land was enclosing them; they must surely be seen at any moment. But so far all was quiet. Just the sound of the wind, and seas breaking, and the ship and engine sounds. Keeping in the wake of his next ahead, Cameron held his ship now to the south of the Goulet, steering a course that would take him between the Presqu'île de Quélern and the shoals in the middle.

It was as they came below Pointe du Portzic and a little north of Pointe des Espagnols and La Cormorandière that the defence showed the first sign of alarm: a searchlight, probing out from the northern shore. The beam wavered; then the leader, *Panoply*, was brilliantly outlined and the searchlight began to travel down the line of advancing destroyers.

'Open fire,' Cameron said. 'Target, the port and the searchlight. Yeoman, hoist the battle ensign!'

He hadn't finished giving the order before *Palatine*'s guns opened, all the 4-inch main armament crashing out in ear-splitting sound and the ship still rushing ahead under full power. Flashes came from the other two; they seemed to be moving through a sea of waterspouts as the Germans opened on them in return. By now three searchlights were in action. One of them dimmed and died as the multiple pom-poms opened from all three ships, but still the port was a blaze of light and there was noise everywhere. The German defence had some big guns – this was known from the recce missions, aerial photography by the RAF. Once they were alongside, those guns would be unable to bear, but for now they were making the most of their opportunity. And they were lethal: the leader, making fast towards the entrance through the breakwater, was almost there when she slewed to starboard as though taken by some giant's sledgehammer, her fo'c'sle buckled and blazing as the result of a direct hit from a heavy-calibre shell. Machine-gun fire, tracer, arced across from the dockside and sliced into her forebridge. As she came across the channel, seemingly out of control, Cameron caught a glimpse of the carnage in the flames. He doubted if anyone could be left alive on the bridge; but he was wrong.

Behind him Burton said, 'Someone's got his wits about him. They're moving astern for the entrance!'

Ahead, *Probity* only just missed cutting straight into the stricken leader. She swung just in time, and grazed past the

48

burning, shattered fo'c'sle as *Panoply* backed in, expertly handled, through the entrance to the inner port.

'Half ahead,' Cameron ordered. Speed was too dangerous now. The destroyer's way began to come off. Bullets sliced across her decks; two men had gone from Number One gun for'ard. Aft there had been more casualties and Pratt and Cleek were busy in the makeshift medical dressing station. Petty Officer Todd was dripping blood from his left forearm but was carrying on. Time enough to see to that later. A minute later they were through into the port. Ahead of them *Probity* had managed to come alongside and *Panoply*, carrying the marine lieutenant-colonel in overall command of the three commando parties, had got her stern hard up against the dock wall. A stench of gunsmoke, of cordite, lay heavily over the whole area. Passing through close-range weapon fire, Cameron brought his ship alongside just ahead of *Probity*. Hands jumped down to take the wires and drop the eyes over the shore bollards and inboard more ratings under Sub-Lieutenant Terry-Jones and the First Lieutenant backed up the wires and hauled taut through the fairleads, then turned them up round the staghorns. In the wheelhouse Chief PO King wiped sweat from his face with a lurid red handkerchief and said, 'Christ, we've got here! Talk about miracles!' And he added, 'Now we'll start praying for more.'

It was just a few moments later that another miracle took place: a man was seen running flat out from the direction of *Panoply*, dodging bullets, leaping over the usual dockyard clutter of coiled ropes, abandoned cable and piles of junk. The miracle was that he made it intact and took a flying jump from the dockside where *Palatine*'s side was scraping against the stone without benefit of fenders or catamarans. He landed in a heap and was assisted to his feet by Stripey Trudge.

'Bit of an 'urry, lad. What's the rush? Got a message, 'ave you?'

The rating nodded, saw an officer coming up, and turned away from Trudge. The officer was Archer. He asked 'What is it?'

'From *Panoply*, sir. Nearly a clean sweep of the bridge, Captain Farnon has been killed, sir – '

'You'd better inform *Probity*. She's next senior.'

'Yes, sir. But the Colonel of Marines, sir, he's bought it too. Major Shawcross – '

'Right, I get you.' Archer was sweating like a pig: the continuing gunfire seemed to have warmed the very air. Turning, he looked along the decks, now crowded with commandos, and found the Major. He passed the report. Shawcross nodded briefly: no time for obsequies, though the dead colonel had been a friend.

He said, 'We go – right away. Colour-Sar'nt – '

A crash of boots. 'Sir!'

'Get 'em over the side, Colour-Sar'nt.'

Mather began shouting. Archer half expected him to march the men off, left-right-left and swing those arms, that man there – dirty boots. But not so. As Mather's harsh voice rang out it had lost its parade-ground formality. 'Off, you buggers – get over the bloody side, jump for it and make it pronto. Keep right behind the Major. And I'll be behind again. Acting as bloody goad.'

Led by Shawcross, the commandos jumped. It didn't take half a minute for the whole face-blackened party to clear the decks behind the tall figure of Shawcross. Knowing exactly where they had to head for, each man carrying a detailed map in his mind, they faded into the thickening gunsmoke, joined the detachments from *Panoply* and *Probity*, a detail from each main party carrying the charges and fuses for the demolition. From the forebridge Cameron heard small-arms and machine-gun fire.

He looked at his watch. He said, 'Not long now.'

At his side Burton asked, 'The *maquis*?'

'Right. If everything goes as planned, that is.' Cameron put out a hand to the binnacle; he felt dazed by the sheer intensity of the gunfire from both sides. Currently the heavy guns were all British, and they were pounding hell out of the dock installations. They were in fact holding back any German advance, but the Germans were keeping up an intense barrage of light stuff, automatic rifles, machine-guns . . . the casualties were mounting rather too fast. Cameron called the wardroom on the sound-powered telephone. A seaman messenger answered.

'All right down there?' Cameron asked, feeling somewhat useless but wishing to know the score.

'Yes, sir. Coping, sir – '

'How many?'

'Fourteen all told, sir. Mostly minor wounds, the doctor says, sir.'

'Right, thank you.' Cameron replaced the handset. Already Archer had reported ten men dead. That number included Petty Officer Stibbs. There were going to be a lot more before they were through this. Cameron felt helpless. What could he do other than sit there and be shot at? There was no question, of course, of the destroyers standing out to sea in the meantime. The commandos might need support; and if the ships did go out to sea, or moved eastward into the wide waters of the Rade de Brest, an area somewhat similar to the Firth of Clyde, they would find it impossible to get back in again for the pick-up. Besides, there was the promised help of the French Resistance . . . Cameron clenched his fists in frustration.

Where were the bloody French?

Suddenly the yeoman of signals shouted something that Cameron didn't catch. He swung round, saw for himself: a German destroyer coming in through the port entry. He passed the order to the midshipman in the director overhead: *'Target right, all guns fire!'*

Midshipman Richards responded fast. The guns swung, pumped out shells towards the oncoming destroyer, which was firing herself, her target being *Probity* in the centre of the line. Things happened very fast: all the destroyers had opened and a shell penetrated the German's side and evidently went smack into her after magazine. There was a vast explosion and a great tongue of red flame shot into the sky. Fire spread quickly, right along the listing deck, and her plates began to glow. There were more explosions and then, drifting on a little way under the residual thrust from the screws that had now gone along with the engine-room, she began to settle aft. Men poured off her fore decks, jumping into a sea that was starting to cover with blazing oil-fuel spilled from her tanks. But she was not finished yet: her close-range weapons raked the upper deck and super-structure of *Probity*. Thinly through the sound of the battle Cameron heard screams and felt an icy shiver. But *Probity*'s company was hitting back hard. Her multiple pom-pom was still in action, blasting the German seamen left on the sinking destroyer's upper deck. From the director, Midshipman Richards watched them die, dropping writhing to the steel decking or falling formlessly over the side to be licked by the burning oil. Richards watched without emotion: he had been case-hardened by the war already. Not yet twenty, not long with his RNVR commission, he had served two years on the lower deck, a lot of it with Malta convoys. Action all the way; and Richards had shone at gunnery, becoming, unusually for an HO rating in line for a commission, a leading seaman and, eventually, acting as director layer in a V and W destroyer – which was why he'd been detailed for the director aboard *Palatine*. He had an ambition: to exterminate Nazis. Nazis he hated: in the late thirties his father and two brothers had been done up by Mosley's blackshirts in east London. Really done up, put in hospital. Richards' father had never really recov-ered, going into premature senile dementia that had turned him into something not far short of a vegetable, doing unpredictable things like dropping his trousers in the street, in public. Richards had been mortified but protective against the only-to-be-expected reactions of passers-by – and of the police, who'd arrested the old man more than once before he'd been finally put away in a mental ward.

So he wanted to kill Nazis and tonight plenty were dying. But not only Germans – that was only to be expected, too. Feeling the spurt of blood zipping past his face, he looked

52

round at his director layer. Slumped, dead as a doornail, face white in the red glare from the explosions of the shells and the burning destroyer. Richards felt no more blood: he believed that spurt had been a dying act, that he'd turned and seen the man die in that instant.

He used his telephone to report to the Captain.

It was as he did so that the French Resistance, better late than never, went into protective action.

Earlier, the responsibility for the delay had been firmly that of Marie Chalandon, code name Clémentine. She was pretty and she was brave; and very patriotic. She was also a flirt and even more coquettish than most Frenchwomen, which was why she had been chosen to divert a German guard from his duty. She was also obstinate and her father, old Marcel Chalandon, also of the Resistance, who with his wife ran a *patisserie* much patronized by the German officers because Chalandon was for ever expressing his admiration for Herr Hitler, whom in truth he detested – old Marcel was on his death bed and Clémentine refused point-blank to leave him. Never mind the war, she said; never mind the British. Blood came first. Her father had never left her, she would never leave him.

She was adamant.

Jacques, who was to lead tonight's diversion, was furious, waving his arms and haranguing, but it was no use. A sin it might be, but he prayed for God to take Marcel Chalandon before it was too late. If he failed to carry out his orders from London he would never be able to hold up his head again – not that he didn't understand family feeling but . . . *merde*! He said it aloud.

Clémentine flamed up at him. 'To use such a word to a woman, it is horrible, detestable – '

'I'm sorry, but – '

'Please, do not distress me further, I beg you.'

Jacques fumed, but evidently some providence was on his side that night. Ten minutes later old Chalandon died. There was fifteen minutes of tearfulness and then La France reasserted its pull. Stiffening herself the girl said, 'I am ready. I will go.' There was a hint of martyrdom in her voice, of a reincarnated Joan of Arc. She looked in the mirror and dabbed at her face. 'The tears,' she said.

'Never mind the tears, Clémentine.'

'But the Germans.'

'Oh, you'll be all right,' Jacques said impatiently. 'You'll look pathetic and the pigs will wish to comfort you – you'll see!'

They set off, with more tears from Mme Chalandon who was being left alone. But she wouldn't interfere: France had a need of her daughter and Mme Chalandon was made of stout stuff, and the British were coming, sent by Winston Churchill himself. Jacques and the girl walked rapidly through the Brest streets, lying low when a German soldier was sighted, for the curfew was strictly enforced. They reached a basement in a part of the town near the dockyard and were cautiously admitted. In the basement were four men, clustered around a radio receiver and transmitter, one that could be disassembled in seconds when necessary. There was also a bottle of wine.

'You're late.'

Jacques explained. Because of the girl's prettiness, not much was said. But there was no time to share the bottle of wine, they must be on their way. The British, Jacques was told, could not be far off. It was just as he said this that Brest seemed to erupt. Heavy gunfire, one explosion after another shaking the cramped cellar until flakes of dislodged plaster came down like snow. One of the men swore: it was very late. But the disorder of the startled Nazi garrison could act in their favour. It did; it seemed, when they emerged circumspectly from the cellar, that all the soldiers, all the arrogant swine in field-grey uniforms, had been withdrawn from the streets, leaving them free, at least for the time being, to be used by their rightful citizens. Full advantages were taken of this. The men and the girl reached their next objective safely. This was a warehouse belonging to a ship chandler in a narrow street right by the docks entrance – the landward entrance. The chandler was also of the Resistance, an old seaman of the French Navy in the Great War. In his warehouse more men waited. There were fifty of them, all armed with rifles. With them also were grenades and home-made petrol bombs and two stripped-down machine-guns of German Army pattern. The men all stood in danger of their lives should they be found. They were not deterred: France must live, and Germany must die. That was more important than individual lives, a point that was stressed sarcastically to Clémentine, at which she flared up. Jacques calmed her down again with soothing words.

Then, losing no more time as the din of explosions and the heat of flames surrounded the dock area, they set out, a small but very determined company of patriots. Word had already filtered through, and had now been reported to Jacques, that the first objective had been secured an hour or so earlier: the radar station. Hauptmann von Arendt would be found in the morning with his throat cut, behind a bush on the station's perimeter, and the rest would be found, if they hadn't been found already by the Nazi swine, dead in the smashed-up litter of their radar sets and communications system.

They moved fast, and openly. They kept their weapons hidden beneath dirty greatcoats or under jerseys and trousers, those that did the latter walking stiffly like men with wooden legs. Near the docks was a German-built barracks, housing the troops detailed as port guard, and this barrack area contained a small arsenal, or at least a magazine and armoury. This was never especially well guarded, unlike the bomb-proof shelters in their half-built state, the shelters that were so important to the Third Reich that they were guarded like the Führer himself. If they had not been, there might have been no need for the British Navy to be involved; as it was, those shelters were simply not accessible to the *maquisards* on their own.

Nearing the barrack entrance Jacques halted his party in cover, keeping them well hidden from the gateway beyond a turn in the street.

'Now, Clémentine,' he said.

The girl went forward, steadily, face set. Because of the delay, because the British were now here and making such an attack, the tactics had been altered at the last minute, back in the warehouse: Clémentine would in all the conditions of sound and fury be unlikely to have much success in diverting the attention of the sentry. Thus he was instead to be swiftly killed. Clémentine went round the corner and moved in an apparently terrified scurry towards the barrack entrance. Cautiously Jacques peered round the angle of the wall surrounding the military area. He saw the sentry swing his rifle to cover the girl, keep it on her as she hurried forward, bent a little as if in self-protection against any flying debris from the embattled port. The sentry halted her and there was conversation. Then Clémentine moved with the most astonishing speed and the German soldier crashed to the ground with his neck broken and Jacques withdrew immediately from the corner.

'Now,' he said.

They were all well practised at this sort of thing: jumping, they hung from the wall, then with agility and silence they heaved themselves up and dropped down on the other side, unseen in the darkness spasmodically broken by flickers from the gunfire, flickers that caused a confusion of shadows. Keeping low, keeping in the cover of the barrack outbuildings, they moved fast, no more than shadows themselves, merging with the disturbed night, heading for the arsenal.

'Jesus Christ!' Mr Cantley's ears sang; a blast of hot air swept over *Palatine*'s upper deck. For a horrible moment the gunner fancied the depth charges had gone up of their own volition, right there behind him, and he must be already aloft in some other world. If so, then it wasn't at all a better one and his expletive had been an unfortunately-chosen one.

He came to his senses: he was still in the middle of a war. 'What the bloody hell,' he said. The explosion hadn't come from any of the destroyers. And now there was a curious stillness; temporarily at any rate, the heavy German gunfire had stopped. He doubled along the deck, making for the ladder to the forebridge and climbing fast.

He spoke to Cameron. 'Any idea what that was, sir?'

'At a guess, Guns, it's the Resistance. They were all set to blow some sort of ammo dump.'

'They were, were they?' Cantley shoved his steel helmet to the back of his head and blew out a long breath. 'Put the wind up me, that did. Let's hope they haven't blown themselves up with it, eh. What's next?'

'They'll be – ' Cameron broke off. Firing had started up again, not the heavy stuff, but rifles and machine-guns. He stared out from the after part of the bridge to where the noise was coming from. Out from a cloud of smoke came running men: Germans. Cameron spoke into the loud hailer. 'Close-range weapons, open when they come past. But watch it – there'll probably be Frenchmen behind them.'

He switched off. The Nazis were in confusion; there was all the evidence of panic. Sustained firing came from their rear, some of them fell, the rest began scattering away from the British destroyers, all three of which had now opened with their close-range weapons. Few of the Nazis lived through it. There must have been upwards of a hundred of them. Now the quay was littered with bodies and the odd man, wounded, trying to drag himself clear of the flying bullets, leaving trails of blood. Then the firing stopped and a ragged line of men in berets was seen advancing, a tall man in the lead holding aloft the tricolour, the red, white and blue of pre-war France. Behind him came another flag, bearing the Cross of Lorraine, personal emblem of General Charles de Gaulle.

'Guts,' Cantley said, almost in awe. 'What those blokes are risking . . . it don't bear thinking about, sir.'

Cameron nodded. A burst of cheering came from the decks of the destroyers and was taken up by the men of the *maquis*. This, Cameron thought, must be the first time they'd virtually paraded as an army, openly, flaunting their colours against the iron fist of Hitler's thugs. This was another reason why the operation had to be a total success. They couldn't let the Resistance down.

Mr Cantley seemed to sense his thoughts. The gunner said, 'Something to live up to now, sir. Wonder how those commandos are making out. There's been firing down that way, I reckon . . . though there's been so much general din and racket it's been hard to be sure.'

'We should know soon, Guns. Time limit was one hour.'

'And too much of that gone already. I wonder what the buggers will bring up now. Against us, I mean. Funny . . . it's gone all quiet. I don't reckon I like that, sir.'

'Nor me. There's only one answer I can see.'

Cameron was conscious of the gunner's close look at his face. Cantley had got there too. The Germans might not see too much point in risking more casualties in continuing the action against the ships, not when they could hold their horses, deploy their undoubted strength against the commandos attacking the bomb-proof shelters – the Jerries must have ticked over about that by this time – and then seal the port across from Le Petit Minou to Pointe des Capuchins, blocking the exit from the Goulet. Back in Barry this point had naturally been made; Sir Ralph Crooke had been ill at ease about it. He'd said that of course they would have to fight their way out, that was only to be expected. A hazard of war, a particular hazard of this particular operation. None of those at the conference had pressed him. It hadn't seemed fair; Crooke so obviously hadn't liked what he'd had to say. It was what he hadn't said that was important, the reading between the lines: all three destroyers were old, their day was long past, it would be more expensive and time-consuming to refit them than to build more effective modern destroyers. *Panoply*, *Palatine* and *Probity* were more than expendable; they were sacrificial.

Cantley swore beneath his breath. He said, 'We're not bloody *meant* to come out, are we?'

6

Not meant to come out: that was putting it rather too harshly. But no one at the Admiralty was going to mind all that much if they didn't. The success of the operation was worth the cost in ancient ships and in flesh and blood too, presumably. Theirs but to do or die: this time – both. Or at best a POW camp in the heart of the Fatherland and the aching grind of waiting helplessly for the war to finish.

It was a grim prospect. Cameron stared down at the dockside. The men of the Resistance had split up and gone aboard the three British ships. On *Palatine*'s bridge with Cameron was a Frenchman who called himself Octavius, a cadaverous elderly man with one eye and a withered arm, a man who had fought at Verdun against what he called the Boches. He told Cameron that all the men wished to be taken out of Brest to England, there to join the standard of Charles de Gaulle. All the men had been specially selected for the operation once the word had come through from London in the BBC broadcasts to the underground. All were single, all were desperate to fight the Boche openly and in French uniforms when one day the counter-invasion started, as it must. All but Octavius himself and one other were young. There was, he said, the woman, Clémentine. She would stay because of her mother, so recently widowed.

'Clémentine . . . the one you said killed the gate guard?'

'*Oui, m'sieur.*'

'She'll have got away?'

The old man nodded, 'Yes, she will have got away.'

'Suppose she didn't. Suppose she was taken inside?'

The man laughed. 'Clémentine, she knows how to defend herself, *m'sieur*, because she has had to learn the hard way. Do not concern yourself about Clémentine. She is brave – and resourceful.'

Still there was the curious quiet. Not even any sounds from the direction of the bomb-proof shelters. It was very alarming – but those were defeatist thoughts. Any minute now, the explosions would shatter the quietness and the commandos would be seen running back for the ships. Cameron looked again at his watch: fifteen minutes to go. If at the end of that time the commandos had not returned or made contact, the British force commander was under orders to send in a party to investigate. If it was found that the operation had for any reason aborted, then would come the time for the ships to make the attempt to break out from the Goulet de Brest, taking off all commandos left alive. Cameron's thoughts went back to the girl, Clémentine.

He asked, 'What'll she do? Simply go home?'

'*Mais oui, m'sieur*. What else?'

'But she won't be safe there.'

'Do not worry about Clémentine, *m'sieur!*'

Cameron didn't say any more; but the girl nagged. He was in no position to assess her actual value to what had taken place, but she'd acted for Britain as well as for France, and she was a woman . . . to leave her in peril would be a hard thought and one that would remain with him for a long time, but he didn't see what he could do about it; strictly, it was not his affair. He paced the bridge for a while, then turned to Archer, who had come up the ladder a few minutes earlier.

'Number One, I'm going across to *Probity*. I want a word with Grey – Senior Officer now. Take the ship, will you? And let me know at once if anyone's seen coming back.'

'Aye, aye, sir.'

Cameron went down to the upper deck and jumped nimbly across to the quay. He found it an eerie experience to be ashore in occupied France, within a stone's throw of the enemy, something that seldom happened to those who fought the war at sea and saw the enemy only as something firing from the horizon, or in an attacking dive bomber, or as a U-boat wallowing in the waves after being damaged by depth charges. He went quickly along towards the next ship in the line and clambered aboard. As in his own ship, all hands were closed up at the guns and other action stations, taut, nervy, fingers virtually on triggers, ready for the next happening, wondering what form the German attack would take. Back aboard *Palatine* there was consternation: the buzz had spread from what Mr Cantley and the skipper had been discussing earlier: expendability. Not that they had said much in so many words, but the actuality was all too obvious. Many hearts sank: in others, in the majority in fact, it brought an even harder determination to fight to the end, do their level best to get back home.

'Sod the bloody Nazis,' Stripey Trudge said. 'They're not stopping me. I'll 'ave their guts for garters first.'

'If they have yours instead,' PO Todd said, 'they'll do for braces as well. Why don't you give over eating for a fortnight or so, eh?'

Trudge was indignant. 'Anyone'd think I was fat to 'ear you, GI.'

'Not 'alf.'

'Bollocks. Look, what d'you reckon the chances?'

'Of pulling off the operation?'

'Of getting out.' Trudge sounded worried all of a sudden.

Todd said confidently, 'We'll get out all right, don't you fret, Stripey.'

'I'm not fretting.'

'No. Maybe not. But there's others that are. Young Spragg for one. I see it in 'is face. So don't go spreading alarm and despondency, all right? Old enough to know better – three-badgemen like you, they're all part of the backbone.' Todd tapped him on his ample chest, too much fat there as well, it was like tapping a suet pudding, no response. 'Spread the word, Stripey: we're the British Navy. We always win, ever since Nelson. Remember Vian of the *Cossack* . . . Evans of the *Broke* in the last lot . . . Kennedy who fought the old *Rawalpindi* to the end a year or so back. Just tell the lads that if you need to.'

'Bullshit.'

Todd said, 'No, it's not. It's fact. The sort of fact that helps. Use your imagination if you've got any. Keep the spirits up and you're half-way home.'

'That's bullshit too,' Stripey said, 'seeing as we're bang inside a bleedin' Nazi port.' Todd gave an impatient jerk of his head and marched away to spread hope elsewhere. Like all Stripeys, Trudge was a perennial moaner, if not as bad as some he'd known in his time. Behind him, however, Trudge was preening himself a little: he'd never been called a backbone before. Well, it was true, of course; all that service experience, and the young ODS always thought he was God even if what he knew best was how to keep out of trouble, how to look busy and efficient when you sloped off to have a burn when you shouldn't, how to guard those three badges that spoke of all those years of undetected crime – crime in a Naval sense – all the loafing and that, what you'd got away with by fooling the officers blind . . .

Backbone, eh!

Better live up to it, perhaps.

Like many gunner's mates, Todd was a good practising psychologist. He wasn't despondent about what he found around the ship. The lads were bearing up well for the most part, however hard it was on the nerves just to be sitting around and waiting to see what was thrown at them. Todd didn't like it himself. The buzz was all too accurate in his view. Stood to reason, they'd be hemmed in. He'd suspected it all the way along but wouldn't say so, not wanting to be an alarmist himself. But of course they would fight through. Just the same, it would have been nice if they'd had something like a cruiser squadron waiting outside to give them the cover of 6-inch guns. But that was wishing for the moon; the poor old *Andrew* was wickedly overstretched and all the cruisers were

63

fully occupied with their own concerns, guarding the convoys
for the most part or acting as escorts for the battlewagons
when they put to sea, which sometimes they did, from the
Firth of Forth or Scapa. To hazard a couple of cruisers, even if
they'd been available, was a different kettle of fish from three
old boats that were being held together by their paint and a
ball of string.

One of the places Todd didn't visit was the wardroom.
Gunner's mates were best out of medical dressing stations
unless they'd copped a bullet or such. In the wardroom LSBA
Cleek was revising his opinion of the quack. Surgeon
Lieutenant Pratt was doing fine. To say he was performing
miracles might not be too far off the target. He'd got his
confidence in full measure, had Pratt, no hesitation at all. His
whole heart was on the job and he had no time over for doubts
or nerves, even though some of his earlier fears were being
realized. Blood in plenty and a good deal of surgery to be
performed. Some of them he knew he wouldn't save, those
with really bad chest or stomach or head wounds, but he was
doing all that was in his power to help them. Cleek was proud
of him. It was a high responsibility to be the sole doctor in the
ship – and the quacks in the other two ships would be just as
fully occupied and no more experienced, probably, than Pratt
– especially when the only available hospital was a Jerry one,
or anyway a French one in Jerry hands.

Ten minutes after leaving the ship, Cameron was back
aboard. He went straight to the forebridge for a word with the
First Lieutenant and navigator.

'No sign yet?'

'No, sir.'

'Five minutes, then. Grey's sending his party ashore to
check as per orders, as soon as the five minutes are up.'

'And us?'

Cameron shrugged. 'Just go on waiting, Number One,
that's all there is to it.' He added, 'Grey's been injured.'

'Badly, sir?'

'Not too good, lost a lot of blood. He's not a youngster,

either. I don't like it.' Cameron said no more, neither did the others, but they all knew one thing: if Lieutenant-Commander Grey died, that left Cameron in command of the group. His function would then change drastically. Instead of obeying the overall strategic and tactical orders, he would have to frame them if things had gone wrong and all lives would be at his disposal for good or ill. To command a ship was one thing and big enough in itself, to decide the whole conduct of a group was another. It meant trying to probe the mind of the Admiralty for one thing, to formulate orders that would be in accord with the intentions of Whitehall, never an easy thing to do since Whitehall was seldom one hundred per cent specific in the first place. Whitehall always liked to have a let-out in reserve: to blame the man in charge on the spot was quite a normal pastime of the mandarins. Everyone was aware of that. Any officer or rating of experience could tell a tale of a captain or an admiral sacrificed so that the infallibility of the Admiralty could be held intact in the public mind. It had started with Admiral Byng, shot by a firing party of his own marines aboard his own flagship in Portsmouth Dockyard in 1757. There had already been Byngs in this war, though now they didn't go so far as to shoot them; they just eased them off into a quiet number somewhere, without hope of promotion.

'Five minutes,' Burton said. 'And still all quiet.'

On the dot, a party of armed seamen was seen to leave *Probity*, jumping down to the quay and moving forward at the double under a petty officer and sub-lieutenant, heading towards the bomb-proof shelters. There had still been no sign of the commandos, no further indication of action from their sector: Cameron was convinced of the worst. He wasn't the only one. Chief ERA Osgood climbed the network of steel ladders that festooned his engine-room, emerged into the open through the air-lock, and found Chief PO Bartlett.

'What's the buzz, Buff?' he asked.

'Sod all. Deathly 'ush. I don't like it.'

'You can say that again. No more do I. Them bootnecks . . .'

'Yes. Too ruddy quiet. They'd have been back.'

Osgood said, 'If they hadn't all been wiped out. Suppose they have, Buff. What then?'

Bartlett shrugged. 'Up to *Probity*'s skipper, isn't it?'

Osgood was about to make some further comment when there was a burst of rapid and sustained fire from the direction taken originally by the commandos. Bartlett said, 'Strewth,' and doubled away towards his action station. Osgood vanished back into the air-lock and down to the starting platform, knowing he'd really had no business to have left it without permission from the forebridge. Already Cameron was passing the orders for the close-range weapons' crews to cover the area where the gunfire had come from. A moment later there came the sound of running feet and then, through the darkness that had descended again after the heavy gunfire had ceased earlier, a Naval rating was seen moving like a bat out of hell. Bullets spattered around him; as he fell Germans were seen behind. From the British ships every close-range weapon opened and Nazi uniforms were seen to crash to the ground. The firing from the Germans stopped. As the British continued to give cover with the Oerlikons and pom-poms, Cameron saw a man jump from *Palatine*'s quarterdeck and, keeping low, run towards the rating, who was trying to drag himself along the quay to safety.

Todd was the man who had jumped. He reached the injured rating, picked him up bodily, and moved back as fast as he could for the ship. Two more men jumped down to his assistance and the injured rating was lifted to *Palatine*'s deck and carried down to the wardroom.

The gunner's mate reported to Cameron.

'Bad, sir. Bullets in the chest and stomach. Doctor reckons he won't make it.'

'Has he said anything, Todd?'

'No, sir. Unconscious when I picked him up.' Todd was himself covered with blood from the dying man. 'But we do know there's Jerries back there,' he added, jerking a thumb

66

into the darkness. 'Lying low for now. Maybe not for long.'

'They'll get a hot reception,' Cameron said. 'And they'll know it. They'll most probably hold back. But – ' He broke off as the sound-powered telephone whined. He took up the handset. 'Forebridge, Captain speaking.' He listened, his mouth hardening, lines deeply etched on his face, visible in the dim glow of light from the binnacle. He hung the sound-powered telephone back on its hook and turned to Todd and Burton. 'That was the doctor. That man's dead. He spoke before he died. The whole party from *Probity*'s been shot up. Walked slap into it.'

'And the commandos?' Burton asked.

'I don't know. That was all he said.'

'Easy enough to deduce, sir.'

Cameron said, 'Yes. Germans in strength. And nothing from Major Shawcross.'

'And no sound from up that way, sir,' Todd said. 'Obvious, I reckon.'

There was a silence. No more Germans showed themselves. Cameron turned away and paced the bridge. All eyes were on him. He believed, they all believed, that the commandos had had it. They could have walked straight into a trap, a very lethal one, right into the German guns. They could all be dead; or there could be prisoners, already being mustered for the rail journey to a camp in Germany. Others might, just might, be in hiding somewhere. Cameron stopped his pacing. He said, 'Yeoman, report by light to *Probity* . . . no, better if we don't use vs. No point in being too open even now.' He sent the bridge messenger instead with a report to Lieutenant-Commander Grey. 'Tell him I'm awaiting orders,' he said.

The messenger clattered down the ladder and jumped ashore, ran like the wind for *Probity* astern. Once again all was quiet, the Germans just biding their time. It was a curious and uneasy sensation, a feeling of suspension in the unknown, the unassessable. Cameron's thoughts were that the whole show had been an appalling flop, that a whole lot of men had

67

died unnecessarily in a hopeless operation, one that should never have been mounted. Somewhere along the line there had been an intelligence blunder; someone should have been better informed of the German strength, of the apparent impregnability of those U-boat shelters. Either the recce boys of the RAF, or the French Resistance themselves, had failed to provide adequate reports. He said this to Burton; the Frenchman, the man called Octavius, took him up on that.

'Very full reports were made, Captain,' he said. 'The full truth was told in our broadcasts. We said to the British, the shelters were beyond the power of the *maquis* unaided . . . then they asked for more detailed information, which we gave. It was the British who made the decision.'

'Yes, I accept that.'

Burton said savagely, 'It's probably a case of pig-headedness in high places. Someone was struck by an idea and forced it through. Like the Dieppe raid. That was just as much of a bloody disaster.'

'Doesn't help us now, Pilot. We won't talk about disasters yet. We're still here.' To himself Cameron thought: so what? Nothing we can do now if we accept, as we have to accept, that the operation's aborted. Except pull out and salvage what's possible, fight our way through, out to the open sea. His heart was in his boots. He didn't like the sour taste of a mission uncompleted, of failure. He guessed Grey wouldn't like it any more than him, but there appeared to be no real alternative. And at least some damage had been done to the port of Brest, and they wouldn't leave without having killed some of the enemy, for what that was worth as a tit for tat. None of it had been worth the loss of British lives . . .

That was what CPO King was thinking, at his station in the wheelhouse, standing by waiting for movement orders and feeling useless in the meantime. He didn't like to see lives chucked away and in his view, though he'd never said so to anyone, this piss-up had sounded a dead duck from the start, as the brass must have known. If the bomb-proof shelters were so vital, as he conceded they were, then the Jerries

68

might have been expected to put a heavy guard on them and likely enough even a couple of battalions of troops wouldn't have been enough to penetrate them. Some people, some high-ups, were dead from the neck up . . . in the meantime King could do with a cup of kye – the thick, glutinous cocoa always simmering in the galley to warm the watchkeepers by day or night. Fat chance of that, though. The skipper wouldn't want any hands to be missing from action stations to go and get it, even though sod all was happening currently. You never knew when the Jerries would start up again. King lit a fag and handed the packet to the telegraphsman, taking the weight off his feet by sitting slumped against the bulkhead in a corner of the wheelhouse.

'Thanks, Chief.' The OD stirred himself to take the offered cigarette, then slumped down again. 'What happens now, I wonder, Chief?'

'Don't ask me, lad. I'm not the fount of *all* wisdom.'

Ordinary Seaman Lappett gave a faint grin. In the short time they'd been together he had got along all right with the Chief, who gave promise of not being at all bad for a coxswain – senior rating on the lower deck of a destroyer, a kind of lower-deck God. But he saw the way he was being looked at now, sort of shrewd, a summing-up look. He knew he'd been shaking like a leaf in a gale for the last hour, since the gunfire had started up. King, on the other hand, as you'd expect, was like a rock, not a nerve in his body by the look of him. Suddenly the coxswain said, 'Don't like this much, do you, Lappett?'

'No, I don't,' Lappett said.

'That's honest. I don't like it either. No one likes it. Shall I tell you something, lad?'

Lappett nodded. King said, 'I'm scared too. All the way. Only a bloody fool wouldn't be. First time I was in action was back in the last lot. Boy Two in the old *Iron Duke*. Jellicoe's flagship – Grand Fleet. Nearly had a nasty accident – very embarrassing.' He changed the subject. 'What was you before you joined?'

'Trolley-bus conductor. Pompey.'

'Pompey, eh? Probably carried me back to the dockyard gates many a time.'

'South Parade Pier to the dockyard . . .' Lappett wasn't really listening. 'Only started the job just before the war.' Glad enough to talk, Lappett began telling the coxswain what life had been like in the corporation trolley-buses. How he'd got along with the girls, the ones who travelled regularly to work and back again, the ones he got to know, the dates that that had led to sometimes; the time, not so long after war had broken out and before he'd been called up, when his trolley-bus had been passing through the Circle in Southsea just as the Nazis had dropped incendiaries nearby, and he'd left the trolley-bus and gone to help put out the fires. He hadn't been scared then; once the bombs had dropped the thing was over till the next time. But now, here in Brest, it was all continuing and there was the terrible uncertainty of not knowing when a projy might come slap through the wheelhouse . . . he was saying this to King when a voice came down the pipe from the forebridge. Not an order: a bit of conversation – a report rather – picked up and wafted below.

King was standing right by the bottom end of the voice-pipe. He said to Lappett, 'Hear that, did you?'

'No, Chief – '

'Captain of *Probity*, he's in a coma. Doesn't know what's going on around him.'

'You mean – '

'I mean the bloody obvious, lad. That leaves the skipper in command of the group. It's up to him now.' He stubbed out his cigarette in the lid of an old tin of Tickler's tobacco acting as an ashtray. 'Best get off your arse and stand by for orders. For my money, we'll be moving out. This job's gone right up the spout.'

7

'There's still the objective,' Cameron said. He'd been shaken at first, in the moment the news had come from *Probity*, but inside himself he'd been braced for it; he was ready to assume the overall responsibility and had been directing his thoughts to that end. 'We came here to blow the U-boat shelters.'

Archer said, 'We came as transport, really. It was always a commando job, sir.'

'Nevertheless, the orders stand.'

'I don't see how we can carry them out on our own, if that's what you mean. For one thing, we haven't any demolition charges.'

Cameron turned to Mr Cantley, summoned to the bridge with the First Lieutenant. 'Guns?'

'I can improvise, sir, but they wouldn't be a tenth as effective as what the bootnecks had with 'em.'

'You mean you don't think you can do it?'

Cantley closed his eyes for a moment: talk about blunt directness! It was true, though, what the skipper had said. 'I don't think I can produce anything good enough, sir, no.'

'What about the depth charges? Can they be utilized in any way?'

'How sir? Use the throwers, chuck 'em at the bloody shelters?' Cantley gave an edgy laugh, no humour in it.

'Not exactly, Guns,' Cameron said evenly. 'Use the explosive in them, was what I meant.' He had an idea Cantley had no ready answer to that one; but for the time being he

71

wasn't going to press. The gunner could brood on it for a while and then come up with his own notions. He said, 'One thing's for sure: we're not staying here, not staying alongside. I've an idea we've outstayed our welcome and the Nazis'll start throwing things at us again, any moment now.'

'So where do we go?' Archer asked, spreading his hands palms uppermost in a gesture Cameron found irritating. 'If we go to sea . . . that means leaving the port, so what about the objective?'

Cameron said. 'Not to sea. Number One. Not so far. We have to think of the commandos. We don't know for certain what's happened. There could be some who got away. There could be wounded.'

'But – '

'I'm not leaving them to it,' Cameron said flatly. He turned to the Resistance man. 'What chance would we have if we moved into the Rade – say the south-west part?'

Octavius said, '*M'sieur*, it would be a trap, much more so than here. It is farther into what are now enemy waters and there is no way out except past here again. On the other hand . . .'

'Yes?' Cameron asked impatiently.

'On the other hand there are friendly people, people of the *maquis*, all well known to me, of course, *m'sieur*. It might yet be possible if the ships remain in the vicinity even to blow up the shelters, which I think you have still in your mind – '

'Yes, I have, but – '

'If there are commandos still alive and free, and with the added help of your sailors, we might yet achieve this. To bring out your ships again might be impossible, but the objective – yes, perhaps, if you are willing to take to the land.'

'And the German presence in the Rade, their Naval presence?'

Octavius said, 'All the ships went to sea as I understand, three days ago now. Destroyers and small craft, what you would call, I think, motor launches and E-boats.'

Cameron nodded. The east coast and Channel convoys

were always coming under attack from the E-boats, fast torpedo-carrying craft. The route north from the Nore in particular was so bad that it had become known as E-boat alley. Brest was a long way south, but the Germans could have sent reinforcements to Hitler's more northern ports – or the convoys passing through the Channel might be coming under attack. Archer said, 'If we can't bring the ships out again – '

'We'll be having a try at it,' Cameron interrupted, 'but the ships themselves are of less importance than what we came to do – we're all conscious of that fact, have been all along. Pilot, can you take us into the Rade de Brest?'

'Enemy action permitting, yes. It'll be tricky off the Ile Longue – Notices to Mariners indicate a number of wrecks off there – RAF bombing – '

'We'll risk it,' Cameron said. 'Messenger?'

'Yes, sir?'

'Nip smartly along to *Panoply* and *Probity*. Inform their First Lieutenants, I've taken over command of the group and propose moving out from here into the Rade, which is said to be free of warships. They're to follow my motions – there'll be no signalling except in an emergency – and they'll leave in line ahead behind me, no further orders. I'll be getting under way immediately you're back aboard. Got all that?'

'Yes, sir – '

'Right, lose no time then.'

The messenger went down the ladder fast, sliding the rails through his hands. Archer, clearly not liking Cameron's decision, left the bridge to see all correct along the upper deck and below. Cantley went down to have a word with the gunner's mate about the conversion of depth charges into demolition charges. Cameron, while Burton laid off his courses for the move into the Rade, called the engine-room. 'Moving within the next couple of minutes, Chief. I take it you're all ready.'

'All ready, sir, yes. Steam at immediate notice as ordered, sir.'

'Right. Stand by main engines.' Cameron moved to the wheelhouse voice-pipe. As he did so he gave a sudden shiver. So many dead already that night; and God knew how many more had their names and numbers on the shells that the Nazis were going to pump towards them when the movement started. The recent quiet had held foreboding and it wasn't going to last much longer.

It was a little over Cameron's estimated couple of minutes before the messenger came back. As he scrambled over the side the chief boatswain's mate had his party ready to nip ashore and take the eyes of the mooring wires off the bollards. The messenger doubled to the bridge and reported the orders passed and understood.

'Thank you,' Cameron said. Taking the ship himself, he bent to the voice-pipe and called the wheelhouse. 'Stand by, Cox'n.'

'Aye, aye, sir.'

'Cast off, Number One,' he called to Archer on the fo'c'sle. The orders were passed fore and aft and the wires came off and were quickly hauled inboard. The engines were put to slow ahead and *Palatine* began to creep off the berth. Aft by the depth charges stood Stripey Trudge having a bit of a loaf, getting his breath back after helping to heave in the stern-line. He was getting old for this sort of thing. As he mopped at his face he saw something streak across the deck from the door in the after screen, something that jumped across to the quay and just made it before the gap between ship and shore widened.

The cat. *The bloody cat*!

Trudge watched in horror as the cat vanished from sight round a pile of junk. Poor bloody object, probably thought it was Barry. Now it was in enemy territory, in bloody Nazi hands, and it didn't know. All his fault, his and Cantley's . . . making such a song and dance about the need to have a cat aboard! Not far short of murder, and what about the luck now? Gone with the cat most likely. Perhaps the cat knew something, had a sixth sense that had told it to bugger off

74

before it had to swim. Reflecting again on his old dad's premonitions, Trudge lumbered to his action station. By ill luck – the start of it? – he encountered the gunner.

'You there, Trudge!'

'Yessir?'

'Was that the cat I saw?'

'Er . . . yessir, I think it was, sir.' Trudge wiped away more sweat. 'Abandoned ship, like, it did.'

'You bloody fool,' Cantley said murderously.

'Not my fault, sir,' Trudge said in an injured tone. 'Cat took it into it's 'ead – '

'Don't argue. You were i/c cat, all right? Fell down on your responsibilities. Poor little sod, should have been shut in somewhere till it got settled down. For two pins I'd wring your neck! You've really gone and torn it now.'

'Sorry I'm sure, sir – '

'Just shut your trap, Trudge, you make me sick.' Mr Cantley turned away, even the back of his neck seeming to show outrage. Trudge muttered to himself, angrily, beginning to blame the cat itself. Stupid little prat, pissing off at the wrong moment. If it hadn't done it within sight of the gunner, Trudge could have wriggled out of it somehow, he was far from unaccustomed to finding excuses, but what was seen couldn't be got out of by any stretch of the imagination. Not fair. What a bleeding life. From now on, when things went really wrong, and they were bound to with all this daft steaming up the perishing Rade de Brest, everyone would put the blame on him, the mucker-up of luck. Trudge, climbing the ladder to the after gun-deck, almost fell down it as there was a flash and a bang from somewhere away to starboard and a projy flew over his head. The Jerries were back to normal again. The ship was all right, but one of the warehouses behind the quay went up in a lurid blaze half obscured by writhing smoke. Daft buggers, the Nazis, destroying their own nicked property. Trudge scuttled up the ladder like an animated sack of potatoes, surprised at his own speed under pressure. He saw that the ship was well off the quay now, and turning for the gap between the breakwaters, and *Panoply* and *Probity* beginning to follow through, *Panoply* going arse-end first on account of her damaged fo'c'sle – she would never make it, not a hope in hell, Trudge thought, not enough speed when going astern.

From the forebridge, Cameron conned his ship for the gap, staring ahead. Closer . . . almost there now. Tracer arced across from starboard, too high until the trajectory was flattened and then it wasn't funny. Cameron felt the impact as bullets zinged off his steel helmet. He heard a grunt of pain behind him but was too occupied in handling his ship to look round. Now they were coming up into the water between the long arms of the breakwaters and a moment later they had the great stone masses abeam.

As Cameron ordered the engines to full ahead everything in the port seemed to open on the three ships – they were back in the heavy fire now, moving out to where the big-gun batteries on the shore could be brought to bear on them. At least if any of the commandos were hidden up somewhere this firework display would give them a chance. Up in the director, Midshipman Richards gave the guns their target: those shore batteries, identified by the flashes each time they opened. A ship under way always had the better of this kind of battle: a moving target was harder to hit. Richards kept very cool, almost icy, and he had a good director layer as replacement for the dead man, who had been hauled out during the lull. As the targets came on, Richards pressed his firing pistol at precisely the right moment. The electric impulses went to the guns and one of the shore batteries erupted. It was something like the London blitz on a small scale: debris and bodies flew and there was one explosion after another and the wind was bringing down a taste of the appalling, blistering heat that was cremating the German gunners alive as the whole sky appeared red with flame.

Cameron passed the word up: 'Well done, Mid! And well done the guns.' A lot of ammunition must have gone up, he believed; and that wouldn't have done the Nazis' morale any good at all.

The ships were now moving ahead fast with the inner harbour behind them. Cameron wiped sweat from his eyes as he passed down a course for entry to the Rade. It might – would – be a tricky passage between Ile Longue and Pointe de l'Armorique until the water widened into the Rade itself. Burton had mentioned the Notices to Mariners: RAF reconnaissance after the bombings had indeed shown a large number of wrecked vessels whose presence would narrow the channel between the arms of the land and seriously impede pilotage for any sizeable ship trying to enter. Cameron glanced astern: *Probity* was nicely away, with the damaged *Panoply* still moving stern first. Away to the west Cameron made out other ships, Germans or Vichy he didn't know, lurking in the Goulet . . . they would have been expecting any break-out to be made that way, somewhat naturally. Cameron grinned briefly: there would be plenty of confusion in the enemy mind now, not that it was likely to last. Turning back, he saw Yeoman of Signals Leckwith staring at something on the deck, and the something was Burton. Leckwith, looking up, caught his eye.

'Lootenant Burton's bought it, sir.'

'Don't just stare at him. Send down to the doctor!' Cameron remembered that low-key grunt. Too much time had been wasted already.

Leckwith said, 'No use, sir. He's dead. Head, sir. It's half gone. Only just seen it.' He moved suddenly for the rail and Cameron heard retching. As he moved over to the port side of the bridge to watch out for shoaling water his foot slipped on blood. There was a lot of it about. Leckwith brought his head back from the rail. He was shaking like a woman in orgasm and he was thinking that all his years of service had never hardened him to this sort of thing, which in any event didn't happen in peacetime. The skipper was standing up to it better and never mind that he was Wavy Navy. Cameron hadn't the time just now to worry about Burton or any others who might have died. He had to concentrate on the passage into the

Rade . . . and he found himself wondering what he was going to do when he got there. Too hasty a decision? But what else could he have done? He still believed there would be some commandos alive and in hiding – men like Shawcross didn't go and lose all their men just like that – and he had a responsibility to them that couldn't be tossed aside. One thing he registered was that the Resistance man, Octavius, was no longer on the bridge with him. Gone below, no doubt – sensibly, in case he was outlined by the searchlights that had come on just before the heavy batteries had opened up.

A little later as Cameron took the ship through between the wrecks there was an explosion astern, a heavy one. More flames lit the night. In a high voice the starboard lookout reported. '*Panoply*'s gone up, sir!'

Cameron acknowledged but didn't look back: all his attention had to be ahead. Yeoman Leckwith gave him a commentary: 'She's settling, sir. Not much left of her. Still burning, though. Christ, them poor buggers.'

In war, men died. Cameron had to harden his heart. You kept to the orders and you aimed for the objective, no matter what, and he passed no order to *Probity* to stop and pick up survivors. You couldn't hazard another ship. But Cameron's heart seemed to contract at the thought of what would happen to those of the Resistance who'd boarded *Panoply* and might now drop into the grip of the Nazis. Beatings, cigarette burns, starvation, degrading conditions, the long-drawn-out tortures in the attempt to extract names, the end of all hope.

Behind Cameron Leckwith said, 'She's half blocked the channel, went down right where it's going to be most bloody awkward for the Jerries, sir!'

Then her company would be fighting for them still. In death they'd performed a service. The Germans might not follow through behind them, preferring to play a waiting game. In the meantime the passage between the obstructions in the entry to the Rade was turning out much less lethal in terms of attack than Cameron had feared. The Nazis had positioned their gun emplacements and their troops solely so as to protect the port itself. It would never have occurred to them, perhaps, to worry about the inshore waters to the south. Only a lunatic would steam into the enclosed Rade. Once away from the actual port area there was nothing to it other than the difficulties of pilotage in strange waters. Those waters would have been strange even to Burton. The great peace-time liners of P & O didn't enter the Rade de Brest. Now, in wartime, there would have been difficulties even for anyone who *had* entered in the days of peace. So much destruction had been caused by British bombs, so many of them over so long a period. It wasn't just off the port itself, in the passage between the headlands; the skeletons of those sunken ships, thrusting up through the water everywhere as it seemed, had made a nightmare of it all.

8

Palatine and *Probity* headed unpursued into the Rade's south-west arm. So much had happened in so short a time: the dawn was not yet with them, though Cameron noted a very slight lifting of the total blackness that showed that it was not far off. His eyes ached from the strain of closely watching out for uncharted obstructions, of conning the destroyer past jags of rusted metal sometimes with only inches to spare as they loomed up suddenly through the dark. It had been touch and go: it would be a sad thought to end up stuck fast to a ship sunk by the RAF.

Cameron, rubbing at his eyes, thought that so far they'd been in luck and never mind the cat deserting. That news had spread fast. Mr Cantley was still muttering about it and had infected the gunner's mate who was going about his duties with a long face and a hard stare whenever he encountered Stripey Trudge. Not that Todd had too much time for cats as such: they made messes aboard clean ships, needed nursemaids with shit pans handy. On occasions, if they were female, they had kittens which was always a perishing nuisance because the Jolly Jacks got all sentimental about them and you had to contain yourself when you heard some horny-handed AB turning his voice to a wheedle and saying 'poor pussy then' or some such tripe and holding out a tit-bit like a dollop of herrings-in or a hunk of corned beef.

So it wasn't that. Oh, no. It was Mr Cantley himself, as Todd said to Trudge. 'Bloody nuisance you are. Got me in Cantley's bad books. Says I've lorst control of the gunner's party. All cos of the cat. I dunno! Some people. Set his heart on a cat, has Cantley. You'd think he'd have grown out of it by now.'

'Shows 'e's a kid at 'eart. Some kid! Got softening o' the brain if you asks me – '

'I don't, Able Seaman Trudge. An' I don't encourage criticism of officers, all right?'

Trudge stared. 'You *just* – '

'Never mind what I *just*, do like I said.'

Stripey recognized the snap of authority, the sudden transformation. Gunner's mates were always like that, and sod them. Stripey said, 'Right-o, GI, just as you say.'

'And don't stand about doing fuck all.'

'No, GI.'

'Take your hands out of your pockets.'

'Yes, GI.'

Todd marched away, left-right-left, arms swinging, another ineradicable habit of gunner's mates under all circumstances. Trudge, who had once been captain of the heads in the battle-cruiser *Renown* – in non-Naval terms, the bloke that cleaned out the lavatories – had seen the chief gunner's mate marching to the door of a cubicle, halting smartly and pausing one-two before opening the door and going inside, where no doubt he had performed by numbers, giving himself the orders as he undid his braces. There was just no accounting for gunner's mates, they were the bane of all seamen in the Andrew.

Just then the bosun's mate came along the upper deck, piping – not an order but information from the bridge. 'Do you hear there! The ship is proceeding to an anchorage. Further action is not expected in the meantime but all 'ands will remain closed up until further orders.' Coming alongside Trudge, the voice lost its official, carrying sound. 'What's up, Stripey? Bust a gut at last, have you?'

'Don't be bloody impertinent to your elders, young Lofty. Just chokka, I am.' Bosun's mates, youngsters mainly, were not in the same category as gunner's mates.

'Yes, and I know why you're chokka.' Ordinary Seaman Brown chuckled. 'Done the ship a bad turn you have.'

'Crap off.' Trudge took a mock swing of his fist. Again, it was all unfair, he was being made a mockery of, a bloody butt for a stupid OD's idea of wit. Brown continued along the deck until Trudge called him back. 'What's the buzz?' he asked.

Lofty Brown stared at him. 'Buzz? No buzz, fact, Stripey. Skipper's gone like Harpic, clean round the bend. Going to anchor the ship and send a party ashore to march south and capture Musso. Then he's going to telephone Hitler and ask him to call off the war in gratitude for – '

'Oh, bugger off,' Stripey said angrily. 'I'm not that daft, stupid little twit!'

Grinning, the bosun's mate went on his way. Stripey thought about a bite of breakfast, but no meal had been piped as yet. *Palatine* and *Probity* moved on and all was peace around them. On the forebridge Cameron was studying the chart and feeling the lack of Burton's competence. This was one of the times when experience counted, and Burton had had a lot more of that than he, Cameron, had. He didn't find his First Lieutenant a lot of help. Archer had had hopes of specializing in signals but hadn't made it. Now he was what was known as a salt horse, a competent seaman but with no specialist qualifications, and he'd already confessed that pilotage was not his strong point. He didn't appear to have a clue about tides and sets and eddies, or about holding grounds and prevailing winds. Nor, naturally enough, had the Resistance man, although he did have the immense value of knowing the country fringing the Rade. Now, he said, 'If it is your intention to make contact with the commandos, Captain – '

'That's the idea, yes.'

'Yes. Then here.' Octavius laid a finger on the chart. 'Here is where I suggest the anchoring should be.'

'Uh-huh. Any particular reason, *m'sieur*?'

'*Mais oui*! A road, not a good one but a road, that will lead back to Brest and the bomb-proof shelters. You can anchor close, I think – '

'Depends on the soundings.' Cameron looked again at the stretch of water Octavius had indicated. The chart showed two fathoms above datum. *Palatine* drew a little short of twelve feet. A squeeze, but it should be just about all right even at low water. The suggested anchorage was across the Rade in the south-eastern sector and there were mudbanks en route that would have to be avoided, notably the Banc du Capelan where the maximum depth was little more than a foot and the water around it was also shallow. However, the south-eastern sector appeared from the chart as suitable as anywhere else in the Rade and the remoteness of some of the rivers and inlets just might give them what they most needed now: time – time to try to reach the U-boat shelters and the remnant, if there was one, of the commando units.

Cameron made his decision. 'We'll head east from here, Number One.'

'Looks like a tricky passage, sir.'

'I'm well aware of that.'

'There's another thing: as soon as there's light enough, we're going to come under air attack.'

'Yes, I've thought of that too. We're committed now.'

Archer's grunted response said that was just the trouble. One very big mistake had been made in not heading for the open sea, said Archer's face, or would have done had there been light enough for it to be seen. Cameron disregarded his First Lieutenant's surliness. He said crisply, 'The likelihood of air attack's one reason why I'm going to try to hide up. It may not be possible, of course. But we'll do what we can, Number One. Understood?'

'Yes, sir.' Archer gave a sigh. Cameron disregarded that too. Their acquaintance had been short – with more than a little surprise, Cameron registered that only some twelve hours ago they had been in Barry – but already he had formed the impression that there was some degree of hostility from Archer, the RN versus the RNVR, the professional being subordinated to the amateur, though in all conscience

Cameron reckoned he'd probably done as much sea-time by now as any RN lieutenant, if not more.

He said, 'Right. First thing's to lighten the ship as much as possible and give ourselves a better chance in the shallows. See to that, please, Number One.'

'Right. What do you want jettisoned, sir?'

Cameron gave a short laugh. 'Easier to say what I *don't* want jettisoned! I know it's unlikely the ships themselves are going to come through this. Virtually everything can go except the ammo, the depth charges and food stores – '

'Leave a trail of junk behind us?'

Cameron shrugged. 'It doesn't make any odds now, they know we're here. Get the jettisoning done pronto, Number One – right where we are now.'

Archer nodded and left the forebridge. Cameron told off the yeoman to raise *Probity* by lamp. 'Make, *Am about to stop engines and jettison gear for passage of shallow water,*' he said.

'Aye, aye, sir.' Leckwith levelled his shaded Aldis astern and made *Probity*'s pennant number. Cameron passed down the order to stop engines. *Palatine*'s way began to come off, and astern of her *Probity* also slowed. The two destroyers drifted to a stop. Below, the First Lieutenant was passing the order to the buffer to get rid of all inessential gear. Bartlett passed the order on to the divisional petty officers and went round himself to check. Hands were released from the guns and other stations for the purpose, ready to double back on the instant if the enemy showed. There would be no advance warning: both ships' radar aerials had been carried away by gunfire earlier. There was plenty of tooth-sucking along the messdecks about the skipper's order; though they could all see the sense of it, their personal possessions were dear to them and Jimmy the One had been explicit that they were not to be spared the axe. Stripey Trudge did the most moaning. He hated parting with anything, he was a regular hoarder and as such the despair of his missus back home. He kept even old socks – you never knew when they might be needed, it was a case of waste not want not. But now everything had to be

84

dumped. Even the smallest, lightest things all added up, like the old woman who peed in the sea, every little helped, the buffer said when Trudge tried to protect a small figurine, not so small that he could shove it in a pocket, seamen's pockets weren't big enough to take more than a packet of fags anyway – a lucky bit of china that he'd bought years ago in Ryde in the Isle of Wight, of a small coloured boy sitting on a po with his trousers down and a look of intense concentration on his dial.

'Bloody pornographic,' Bartlett said.

'Tisn't, Buff.'

'What is it, then? Art?'

'Yes, that's it, art.'

'My arse. It goes, Stripey.' Chief PO Bartlett moved on, eyes everywhere. Soon the messdecks were stripped down to almost nothing. Mess tables, lids wrenched from the immovable wooden lockers that acted as seats at the tables, the hammock netting, the mess traps of bread barge and so on, spitkids – all went over the side along with the ratings' and officers' personal gear, everyone left with just what he stood up in. The furnishings from the officers' cabins, the contents – the non-medical contents – of the wardroom and pantry joined the savage defoliation of the ship. All the fittings from the galley, inessential deck equipment and engineer's stores, nothing was sacred. Even the gunner's store was stripped right down, contributing quite a lot of weight to what had become gash for disposal. Last to go was the port anchor and its cable: just the starboard anchor would be all that was needed now. The anchor was lowered to the waterline and then the cable was knocked off the Senhouse slip in the cable locker and both anchor and cable vanished with a roar and a cloud of rust. All in all it gave the *Palatine* another four inches off her draught. Enough, as the buffer said, just to make all the difference in a tight corner.

The First Lieutenant reported to the forebridge. 'Dumping complete, sir. Even the ratings' ditty boxes,' he added in reference to the small wooden chests in which seamen customarily locked their most cherished possessions, transporting them from ship to ship in their canvas kitbags. It had been the ditty boxes that had caused the most heart-searching and adverse comment, especially among the active service ratings and the fleet reservists. A man's ditty box became a friend, something ever familiar to accompany his career, a link with previous ships and with old shipmates. No one parted with them easily: the only things lockable they had – the lockers in a destroyer were misnamed – they became intensely personal, the sort of item that an old salt would like to pass on to his son. One who didn't mind much was Leading Seaman Cusson. His ditty box was a new issue, last time in RNB. A big black rat on board his last seagoing ship, the old cruiser *Vindictive* in Freetown, Sierra Leone, had gnawed his old one to fragments in the course of one night, being caught in the act when Cusson came off the morning watch.

Cameron said, 'Right, Number One.' Already the buffer had reported the reduced draught. 'We'll get under way. I'll want the whaler sent away to take soundings ahead. Terry-Jones can go in charge.'

'Aye, aye, sir.' Archer paused, then went on with something curious in his tone, something that held loftiness mixed with an inflexion of forebearance. 'The CBS, sir. Confidential books. And recoding and recyphering tables. Aren't they at risk of compromise if the Jerries get us?'

Cameron drew in his breath sharply. Archer thought he'd got him this time, that was obvious, and such an attitude was unwelcome in anyone's second-in-command. He said, 'I didn't tell you, Number One. But I would have thought you'd have realized. We didn't bring any codes or cyphers. All we've got is the FSB and the AVSB. Think it out for yourself.'

Archer stiffened. Had there been more light his deep flush would have been visible. He'd made a fool of himself: of course, no ship with *Palatine*'s mission would be given a full set of secret signal publications that could so easily fall into enemy hands. The Fleet Signal Book and the Auxiliary Vessels Signal Book had a low security grading, but the others . . . off the quay in Brest they would never have had time to burn the material and if they had jettisoned it in weighted and perforated canvas bags, the Germans would have dredged them up – it would have been routine to make a search of the harbour bottom.

With an edge to his voice Archer said, 'That means we're considered even more expendable than I imagined.' He turned on his heel and went down the ladder to pass the order for the whaler to be put in the water. Cameron shrugged, awaited the report from the whaler and when it was pulling ahead he got the ship under way again. There was a little light in the sky now, but not much; it was going to be a very dirty dawn. But any lifting of the night's darkness was a help to pilotage and Cameron was thankful for it.

As the ship began to move, Archer looked at the sky from the upper deck. He couldn't see much yet, but he believed there was a good deal of overcast. A nice, thick, heavy blanket. Cameron's luck: they just might not be picked up yet if that overcast was low enough to make the Nazis think twice about an air search. It might be salvation – temporarily – for the RNVR, for a wrong decision. For all their sakes, Archer hoped so, though there was a devil in him that wanted Cameron to be proved wrong in his handling of the operation after the mantle of overall command had dropped on him. Cameron had been right in seeing professional jealousy vis-à-vis the RNVR in his First Lieutenant's manner. Archer had been at Dartmouth, very much the élite. A year or so before the outbreak of war he'd been a snotty in the Mediterranean Fleet, midshipman of the Commander-in-Chief's barge aboard the battleship *Queen Elizabeth*, and you could hardly get a better snotty's job than that. It had meant command at the age of eighteen – not bad going! Command had been manna to Midshipman Archer but he didn't often dwell on it now because it hadn't lasted. Archer had suffered under a difficult executive officer, an officer of commander's rank who had caught him out more than once seeing to his own well-being before that of the barge's crew – always first inboard over the lower boom, the commander had said icily, in dereliction of his duty.

Well, why not? He'd had a first-class coxswain, a chief petty officer of many years' experience who didn't need to be told what to do. The commander hadn't accepted that, though. That wasn't what officers were there for. The result of that and certain other things was that Midshipman Archer had left the flagship in due course with a somewhat poor flimsy from his captain; and flimsies – character references written in the captain's own hand on a piece of paper no thicker than a sheet of bumph – tended to follow a regular officer throughout his career. So Archer had a chip on his shoulder. And it had grown worse since his appointment, fortunately not likely to be a long one, to the *Palatine*.

As things now stood, that appointment looked as though it might end at any moment. The less weighty matters of personal prestige faded as aircraft sounds came from the direction of Brest, approaching fast.

Archer's stomach loosened. He didn't like aircraft attack; he'd had too much of that when taking convoys through to Malta. He had nightmares about the terrible screaming sound made by the dive-bombers. Ack-ack was mostly useless, a matter of luck. You just stood there and waited.

Away behind the approaching aircraft, still in Brest and not yet arrested by the Gestapo, the girl Clémentine who had despatched the German sentry so expeditiously had lost no time thereafter. She had been off and away, a shadow flitting through the night, putting distance between herself and the racket from the port before turning back towards home. She had found her mother still weeping over the body of her father. Clémentine herself was now more philosophical. It was better for her father to have died peacefully rather than to have fallen one day into the hands of the Gestapo when he would have been cruelly tortured. She tried to put this point of view to her mother but without success. Her mother was distracted – such was natural, of course. But there were things to be done.

She said, 'We must go now.'

'Go, Marie?' her mother said, using the girl's own name. 'Why? And go where?'

'As to why,' Clémentine said. 'It is because what the British came to do has not succeeded . . . and now the Boches will be taking their revenge, and all the *maquis* is in great danger.' She spoke with precision as though there was no argument about it. 'As to where, this is obvious. We must go to my uncle in Port Launay.'

'To Henri?' There was amazement in the answer. 'Your father would be so angry – '

'Never mind,' Clémentine said firmly. 'Uncle Henri, he is a pig and a Boche-lover, yes, but because of this we will be safe in his house. He is trusted as a good Vichy man. And remember, he knows nothing of our connection with the *maquis*. So we will go to Uncle Henri's house, taking the road round the Rade. There we shall be safe, and ready for when I am wanted again.' For a moment she took her mother in her arms. 'Come, little mother – courage!'

9

All hands who had been stood down for the jettisoning operation were back at their stations. Cameron listened to the aircraft sounds as they came closer, menacing sounds that were keeping low above the overcast.

He said, 'Fight the ship if necessary, Number One. I'm leaving it to you. I've got my hands full if we're not to go aground.'

Archer understood that: a moment's inattention amidst the mudbanks and that would be their lot. He studied the lightening sky through binoculars: no sign of an aircraft though they were there all right. The overcast was heaven sent, but it wouldn't last for ever. Long enough perhaps, that was the only hope. It was running through his mind that Cameron could always use the W/T – the Germans knew they were somewhere in the Rade and no security would be lost. The PO Telegraphist could use his key and call C-in-C Portsmouth, or the Admiralty or wherever and spell out their predicament in plain language in the absence of the Naval code books . . . but that was no more than a pipe dream. There simply would not be any co-operation.

Amidships the HA armament was ready, the 4-inch barrel moving as it followed the sounds above. The gunner's mate stood by, jaws moving rythmically as though chewing on gum, which he wasn't: it was no more than a kind of reflex action and he was unconscious of it. As the sounds moved away towards the south, Todd relaxed. Like Archer, he didn't go much on being bombed, or machine-gunned from the air either. The way the goggle-eyed bastards came down on you, raking the decks, pock-marking the paintwork, bullets ricochetting everywhere. Todd had been off Crete in 1941, in Lord Louis Mountbatten's flotilla. That had been something he would never forget. Jerry aircraft by the million it had seemed like, all intent on killing PO Todd and everyone else. They'd largely succeeded though Todd was still around to tell the tale. Aided by Lord Louis, God had performed many a miracle off Crete, bringing the surviving British seamen back from the dead almost. He was going to have to do something similar here in the Rade de Brest, this time without support from Lord Louis. Todd walked for'ard, thinking about the skipper on the bridge. You couldn't fault his nerve, but Todd reckoned he'd made a right balls by coming into the Rade. On the other hand, you couldn't just piss off out and give no thought to those marine commandos. Really, the skipper had been caught in a cleft stick. Like the skipper, they had all to make the best of it. But Todd didn't see many of them coming out alive.

Palatine was moving on, dead slow behind the whaler. From the fo'c'sle, Todd looked aft. *Probity* was just visible two cables astern, creeping along in the water disturbed by *Palatine*. There was, Todd saw, a good deal of mud being churned up. The skipper, he was cutting it very fine, very fine indeed. If they were attacked now, they wouldn't have a hope in hell. No room to manoeuvre, no possibility of cramming on speed to dodge the Jerry bombs, not in shallow water. Todd knew very well what destroyers were liable to do: if you went ahead fast in the shallows, the screws had the nasty habit of sucking the water away from under you so that your stern went down. Going down, it bumped the ground and that was that. Twisted screws and your arse well and truly in the mud – or rock, if the bottom was rock.

His attention coming back for'ard Todd caught the eye of Sub-Lieutenant Hope. 'All right, sir?' he asked.

'Still here, GI.'

'That's the spirit, sir.' Todd looked critically around

Number One 4-inch. 'No troubles, have you, sir? Gunwise?'

Hope shook his head. Todd moved aft. Hope resumed his watch of the sky, prayed that the kindly overcast would last and go on lasting. He prayed that he would come through this. He was thinking of home; he was not all that long married. His father had said he was too young but they'd already jumped the gun and Angela believed she'd been caught. The honeymoon had been spent at the King's Head in Masham, on the fringe of Wensleydale in the North Riding of Yorkshire. It had been a wonderful week. They did a lot of walking, all through Coverdale and into Wensleydale, long days in the sun, taking the distances in their stride, literally, looking at splashing waterfalls visible from the road that led from Wensleydale down through Starbotton to Grassington where they bought many varieties of toffee and fudge from a shop called Toffee Smith. It had been in West Witton, in a pub called the Wensleydale Heifer, that Angela had con-firmed that she was pregnant . . . he recalled that now, in the overcast Rade de Brest, recalled it with a pang: he'd said at the time that Heifer was appropriate in the circumstances of her revelation and she hadn't liked his sense of humour; it had led to the first row, nothing monumental, but he wished he'd never said it. They'd finished their drinks in a somewhat frigid silence and had walked down the road towards Leyburn, turning off up a very steep road that led through Melmerby and on by devious narrow tracks with a bit of cross-country climbing as well that brought them down into East Witton on the Ripon road. Angela had seemed tired and they'd been glad enough to get a lift on a brewer's dray going through to the Theakston brewery in Masham.

That had been a little over eight months ago. Two more weeks . . . Hope felt icy fingers grip his spine. Anything could happen in a fortnight, and looked currently like happening in very much shorter time than that. Angela had been in a very depressed state when he had been recalled so suddenly from his next leave to join the *Palatine*, a pier-head jump if ever there was one. She was worried about the future and the coming baby and the fact that she would be on her own when it was born, neither of them knowing that the *Palatine* was under orders for what should have been the shortest of short trips, just across the Channel and back. She'd been really distressed.

Aircraft sounds again.

Hope shouted a warning up to the forebridge. Archer acknowledged. 'Right-o, Hope. Heard it.'

Gnawing fear came back to Sub-Lieutenant Hope, fear and an anxiety like Angela's for the future. Perhaps the old man had been right: war was no time to have the added worry of a pregnant wife. Hope settled his steel helmet more firmly on his head and pulled his white anti-flash gear tighter about his face and hands.

Suddenly the note of the engines overhead changed. It seemed like a falter, a cut-out, then a resumption followed by a curious spluttering sound. The noise veered away to starboard, then came back. Hope heard Archer's shout: 'All guns stand by!' On the heels of the order Hope saw a sudden dramatic blackening of the overcast immediately above the fo'c'sle, a blackening that developed in an instant into the wing of an aircraft, then the body and the engine. Hope did the first thing that came into his head: he yelled unnecessarily at the for'ard guns' crews to get their heads down and then went flat himself.

Ashore to the north during the dark hours of the night the two women had made their way out of Brest, concealed and confined beneath a false floor fitted to a motor hearse. Above them lay the coffin containing the body of Marcel Chalandon: they could hear shifting sounds as the hearse negotiated roads made hazardous by the bombing of the RAF. It was a most terrible journey and in fact at one stage Mme Chalandon's tears had been heard as they were stopped by a patrol of German soldiers and the end had very nearly come for them. However, Pierre Duhamel the undertaker was a resourceful man and so was his assistant Robert Ferrand; and when the hearse was stopped at gun-point as it moved through the dereliction of the Brest streets away from the dock area where all the real German attention was concentrated, Duhamel and Ferrand simply got obediently out of the front compartment of the hearse and stood very still and watchful while they were questioned. Luckily the sergeant in charge of the patrol knew Duhamel, having stopped the hearse on a number of occasions, and was easy.

He asked 'Where are you going this time?'

'To Port Launay.'

'Where in Port Launay?'

'To the home of the brother of the corpse.'

'The one now in the hearse?'

'Yes,' Duhamel answered.

The sergeant guffawed. 'Special meat delivery! And a cold night to do it – I feel snow in the air.'

'It is very chilly,' Duhamel said. He knew the sergeant was about to let them go on; but first the back of the hearse had to be opened up so that the sergeant could clamber in and examine the corpse. Duhamel, knowing well the habits of the Boches, had not yet screwed down the lid. As the sergeant went in, that was the moment Mme Chalandon gave way to her grief, involuntarily but not soundlessly. The soldiers of the patrol – there were three of them all told – stiffened. The sergeant climbed out of the hearse. They all stared at Duhamel. The undertaker, cool as a cucumber from the market, widened his eyes and called out over their heads in French, something about getting the *cochons* . . . and the *cochons*, stupid as any German, fell for it magnificently.

They all swung round as one, away from Duhamel and Ferrand, who brought out automatic pistols, fitted with silencers, and peppered the Boche from behind. As the riddled bodies fell, the undertaker and his assistant banged the rear door shut and then made sure all the Germans wouldn't talk by putting another bullet into each of the heads. Then they got back in front of the hearse and drove away fast. It was a very uncomfortable journey for the two women after

94

that but they reached Port Launay in perfect safety and were taken to Henri Chalandon's house to break the news about poor Marcel and ask for accommodation. Until after the funeral at all events.

Henri Chalandon, always a grouchy man, was sour about it. 'Why do you bring my brother here?' he asked.

Marie answered for her mother. 'The family – '

'Yes, yes, the family. I did not get on with my brother. This you know well.'

'But you are my uncle. We ask for help in a time of grief.' Marie knew, certainly, about the bad blood, but knew also that Uncle Henri was never made aware of his brother's sympathies and had no reason that she knew of ever to suspect them. 'Families should come together at such a time.' She wiped away tears.

Henri Chalandon grunted irritably. 'What's wrong with your own house? Can't you go back there, Marie?'

'Yes. That we shall do. After the funeral. Is it too much to ask, that you give us your hospitality for a few days?'

With a bad grace he gave in. He had room and to spare, having no family of his own. But they were not going to make a holiday of it. Port Launay was a fine little place for a holiday, at any rate in the summer, with its superb position fronting the waters of the Aulne river, with its little quay . . . but he would most certainly not keep his sister-in-law and niece until the soft airs of summer came back to Port Launay – *mon Dieu, non!* He wasn't made of money. As he grumbled his way in behind them, piggy eyes glittering with annoyance, he asked them about what had been going on in Brest, such an amount of gunfire had echoed and rumbled across the Rade, very distant but unmistakable, and a different sound from that made by the bombs from the British aeroplanes. Marie shrugged and said they didn't concern themselves except with keeping safe and they didn't know what had been going on – what with Marcel's death and all that. But it was the British, was it not? Oh yes, it was the British. Such pigs, said Uncle Henri; Marie agreed. They should stay in their stye, it was wicked to disturb the good people of Brest. They were all murderers; Winston Churchill was said to drink blood for breakfast and had grown fangs like a vampire because of it. All so vile. But the Führer was their good friend, who wished only peace. As I do myself, thought Uncle Henri to himself as he told his two women to prepare the bedrooms for themselves and had his brother's body driven round to a patch of ground scratched up by chickens outside his back door. Duhamel and Ferrand were directed to a hostelry in the village. No reason to provide for them.

Aboard *Palatine* there had for a while been total confusion. The aircraft with its stalled engine had come down smack on the fo'c'sle, right on the eyes of the ship and across the cable running to the remaining anchor. There it hung and blazed furiously as the high-octane aviation spirit went up. There was a man alive in the tail – Cameron saw that in the instant before the whole tail end broke away and sagged down into the water in front of his bows. He stopped engines. Archer ran down to the fo'c'sle where fire seemed to be running everywhere. Hope was staggering about with a blank look but was otherwise all right. Dead and wounded seamen littered the burning deck. The buffer came for'ard at the rush, accompanied by the fire parties with their canvas hoses and foam extinguishers.

Cameron felt the heat, blasting back in waves over the forebridge. His nails dug into his palms: he wouldn't hurry men who were doing their best but he prayed they'd get that fire out pronto – it was going to be a dead give-away to anything German or Vichy in the vicinity, not that they weren't going to stand out like a sore thumb before long in any case.

He called down to the First Lieutenant. 'Number One, can you get that German fished aboard?'

Archer waved and called out to the buffer. Able Seaman Matthews was detailed to tend a line over the side, right for'ard or as near as he could get.

'I'd let the bugger sink, Buff,' he said sourly.

'Me too. But the skipper wants him so we do our best, right?'

'Wants him, does he! What the sod for?'

'Hostage, p'raps. Exchange him for bloody Hitler.'

Very funny, Matthews thought, and got his line over with a lifebuoy attached. Some hope: the Jerry wouldn't be able to get out of the tail most likely. But the Jerry did. Wild-eyed in the increasing light of day, he came out through the shatter of the broken back, stood for a moment looking around, then went in and swam for the line. He got a grip and hung in the lifebuoy looking bewildered and Bartlett gave Matthews a hand to haul him inboard. Once up, he shivered as if he was in a state of shock, which he probably was, but Bartlett gave him no chance to be too sorry for himself. He and Matthews dragged him aft, away from the flames that were now coming under control of the fire parties, and got him with a foot on the bridge ladder.

'Climb, you bastard,' Matthews said with a devilish grin on his face, a face that was showing blistering from the fires' heat. *'Up ladder, mate!'* He shoved and the Jerry moved up, still shaking uncontrollably, and reached the bridge where he was confronted by Cameron.

Cameron looked him over. He appeared to be in his early twenties if that. Equivalent of a sergeant rear gunner by the look of his uniform and his position in the aircraft. Cameron asked if he spoke any English: the response was complete collapse. The man seemed to crumple into a heap on the deck of the bridge, without a sound. Cameron bent and felt for heartbeats, then straightened.

'He's still alive,' he said. 'Wardroom, pronto!' The German was made more comfortable while the medical dressing station aft was contacted by sound-powered telephone and a Neil Robinson stretcher was sent up. Matthews was one of the hands who carried the strapped-in German below. In the meantime the burns cases had also been taken to the wardroom and the place looked like chaos, but the doc and LSBA Cleek seemed to be coping. Some of the burned men were yelling blue murder, others were still and silent and white-faced where they weren't purple from the fire – the aviation spirit had spurted a bit and few of the men at the for'ard armament had escaped. Pratt and Cleek had plenty on their hands, Matthews thought, and sooner them than him, he wouldn't never have been able to take it – the cries, the desperate faces, the stink of antiseptics and ether, the hypodermics needling pain killers into veins or whatever – Christ, Matthews thought, it was bad enough when you lined up at the barracks sick bay for the routine jabs of TABT, cholera, and yellow fever if you were going down that way. He escaped back to a sane world or anyway a non-sick-bay one with a sense of relief that he hadn't yet been put in there himself. Yet being the operative word. No, it wasn't a sane world, was it hell, it was a world gone stark staring mad. Matthews went back to the fo'c'sle, where the dead were being removed, taking their turn after the injured but still living. He landed that job as well . . . and a nasty one it was. Seven of the hands had bought it and they were a mess: parts of aircraft had landed on some of them and mangling was hardly the word. Matthews felt sick but carried on and tried not to think about it – until he overheard what the GI was saying to Cantley.

'Problem now, sir.'

Cantley ticked over as to his meaning. 'You can say that again, Jack. No water deep enough for bloody miles.'

'Never been in this sort of situation before. You?'

'No, never. I dunno . . . won't keep for ever even though it's winter and perishing cold. Skipper may have some ideas.'

'I don't see,' the gunner's mate said worriedly, 'what ideas he *can* have. Can't really run burial parties ashore, not in enemy territory.'

'Enemy-*held* territory. Frogs are on our side!'

'Some are. But . . . only thing I can come up with is the beef screen, sir.'

'Along with the lads' dinners?'

That was when Matthews was almost sick over the side. Just to think about it – best not to. Then he noticed a seaman with a gash down one cheek as deep and gaping as a whore's . . . Matthews gave an involuntary gasp of laughter, more like a choke because it wasn't really funny, not this morning, but the rating happened to have a beard and the simile was pretty apt.

They got the bodies down the ladder off the fo'c'sle and ranged them amidships, along the iron deck beneath the funnels. By this time the ship was under way again with the wreckage cleared off the bows and the damage being totted up by the First Lieutenant and the buffer. It was not as bad as it might have been. The guardrails and stanchions had been flattened and the port Blake slip, empty in any case of its jettisoned cable, had been buckled into uselessness. The guns had escaped damage and *Palatine* was fully seaworthy. By now the dawn was up, as dirty a one as Cameron had forecast; the rain had started, sheeting down blindingly as it was blown along a freshening wind from the north-east. All hands along the upper deck, on the forebridge, at the exposed gun positions, felt the icy trickles down their necks as the rain was blown into their faces. In the director Midshipman Richards, who couldn't move around much in his bird's-nest of dials and telephones, switches, buttons and power cables, cursed the weather's discomfort and his current situation. Like the rest of the ship's company he saw no prospect of getting out of a very nasty predicament and it looked as though the Nazis had them now, all ends up. A determined attack by aircraft and that would be that. Finish.

But I'll take quite a few with me.

There was a short laugh from his director layer, Leading Seaman McNee, a dark, wiry Scot with oddly bright eyes. 'That's the ticket, sir!'

'Hell. Did I speak aloud?'

'Aye, you did that, sir. And I reckon I think the way you do. We've bloody had it.'

'I didn't say that, McNee.'

'No, you didn't,' McNee agreed, but he knew that was in the middy's mind all right. As a thought, it was inescapable and in fact McNee had composed himself to accept it, to accept that he wouldn't be seeing Scotland again. Except maybe from above, hovering over the little Perthshire town of Aberfeldy in spirit form like an autogyro, covering the distance from Aberfeldy to Killin in much faster time than he'd ever made it by bicycle along the road running alongside Loch Tay under the shadow of Ben Lawers. He knew that road very well; his parents lived in Killin and his girl lived and worked in Aberfeldy, a waitress in the Breadalbane Arms Hotel where sometimes when on long leave he'd helped out himself in the bar which meant that if they were circumspect about it they could manage a quick cuddle outside the gents, which was opposite the kitchens. McNee wondered how Morag would take it when the telegram reached Killin and his mum or dad passed the news on. He believed she would bottle it up and then in the end go and have a decline, or a breakdown, or whatever it was the quacks called solitary grieving. A crazy thought came to him: he'd like to give her the news himself so that he could comfort her. Maybe it wasn't so crazy. McNee had ideas about the after life, which he believed in very firmly. You certainly didn't cease to exist, you just shifted berth to another plane and carried on, and you could communicate if the will was there on both sides. No reason why he shouldn't be there with her when she got the news, but whether or not he could comfort her – that was another matter; to his sorrow, Morag didn't share his views. She would never know he was there handy. He'd done his best but he'd never succeeded, which was odd really, because Morag never missed a service at the kirk and you'd have thought the minister would have got through to her, but no.

They'd talked about it quite a lot. 'I'll be here with you,' McNee had said one day as they were walking up the Moness Burn, through the trees to where Rabbie Burns had sat on a stone seat and composed the song he'd called 'The Birks of Aberfeldy', there among the birches above the rushing stream, 'if anything happens one o' these days. Which it may.' She held him tight as though she would never let go. He told her once again his theory about the hovering autogyro. 'I know well I'll see it all again, both of us will after we're gone from this life, Morag. We'll climb the Birks, and we'll go along all the old roads again . . . to Grandtully, or down to Kenmore, or over to Kinloch Rannoch – you'll see.'

She'd given a shiver; she didn't like such talk. To her it was gloomy, but it wasn't to McNee. It was something to look forward to, something that gave meaning to the present existence on earth. It was freedom. To have the ability to go at a moment's notice to wherever your heart called you without having to pedal or wait for the bus, and meet everyone you'd known just by bringing them to mind, what could be better? These thoughts grew stronger and more real when McNee took a dram, stronger again after another dram, but he knew they were not the result of drink at all. The drink merely released something in his mind that put him more in touch with that exalted plane that awaited him. He couldn't make Morag see any of it. Nor could he ever have explained to her how he would be with her for ever after he died, and that in the end she herself wouldn't so much die as merge back into a shared life. She'd made some comment about ghosts. Well, all right, maybe that did explain ghosts, plenty of whom were very well authenticated by sober persons. There could come a moment when the planes crossed, or made contact of some sort before they skidded off on their separate courses again. As his mind wandered off down the Birks and across the Crieff road and then past the war memorial at the entrance to the lower part of the burn just opposite the Breadalbane Arms, there was an interruption.

Richards said, 'Hear that, McNee?' He was already calling the forebridge.

Aberfeldy faded on the instant. 'Aye,' Leading Seaman McNee said, 'I do. The buggers are back.'

There was a distant throb of aircraft engines. But the overcast was still there protectively in spite of the wind and

McNee didn't think the moment of exit had come just yet. That was another thing: he believed he would get a warning and that it would come in two parts: signal at the dip, a sort of stand-by, then finally the flag hauled close up for the executive. He had already had the stand-by; but the Almighty wasn't quite ready with the executive. McNee looked down at the forebridge. The skipper was scanning the lowering skies through his binoculars and the warning had now been passed to the guns.

Below, Cameron said, 'There's a pink look in that overcast, Number One.'

'Snow,' Archer said. Silently he prayed that if it was snow it might come soon. The throbbing sounds were coming closer and they might not have long to go. The flames from that crashed aircraft could have pierced the overcast for just long enough; their position, or near enough, could now be known to the Nazis.

10

Earlier, just after *Palatine* had moved through into the Rade and Octavius had come back to the bridge, Cameron had asked him what the Resistance back in Brest would be doing: would they, for instance, try to contact Whitehall by radio and pass the report of failure? Octavius had said yes, they would, but not until they considered it safe to do so and he couldn't say when that would be. It would be up to Control. In any case Cameron knew that when the group failed to make its ETA in Barry Roads the alarm would go up from the Naval Officer In Charge. From then on it was anybody's guess what the Admiralty or the War Cabinet might decide to do. But they wouldn't be expected back yet.

In point of fact the *maquis* in Brest had passed a message within two hours of the abort. As the ships' companies of *Palatine* and *Probity* listened to the throb overhead the Brest message was received in a tall house in Knightsbridge, SW1. The radio operator brought it at once to the attention of the duty officer, who deciphered it and then rang through on the internal telephone to a bedroom one floor up.

He said, 'Operation Scatter aborted, sir.'

'Christ. I'll be down.'

Within the minute a big man entered in a dressing-gown and pyjamas. He held out a hand for the transcribed radio message and with the other put on a pair of gold-rimmed glasses. He sat heavily in a swivel chair behind a massive desk carrying three telephones, one of them coloured red, a lamp, a silver-backed blotter, an intercom and an ashtray. He lit a cigarette, inhaled deeply, blew smoke out and read. Then he said, 'Christ,' once again and looked across at the duty officer.

'Couldn't be worse if it tried, could it, Freeman?' No answer: the question had been rhetorical.

'You'll pass it on right away, sir?'

'Of course, why ask? You know whose idea this whole thing was. Damn and blast!' The big man took up the receiver of the red telephone and pressed the scrambler button. He dialled a number that started with double 0 and was followed by a single digit. It was answered immediately. 'Cabinet Office?' the big man asked curtly. 'Operation Scatter ballsed up. Yes . . . yes. Some commandos believed in hiding, whereabouts not known. Most of 'em dead or badly wounded – walked bang into it, could have been a leak but that's guesswork. No damage to the U-boat shelters. *Panoply* a total loss, all hands killed or captured. Farnon killed on entry. And here's the crunch: *Probity* and *Palatine* have entered the Rade de Brest and are believed to be under attack. Pass on – most immediate.' He added, 'I'll be available instantly when the shooting starts from the old man,' then banged the receiver down on its rest. To Freeman he said, 'Believed to be under attack my backside. *Of course* they'll be under attack. Poor buggers! But what a crazy thing to do. Though I do understand what might be the reasoning behind it. Get me some coffee, Freeman. Black. Hot. Plenty of sugar.'

Freeman nodded and pressed a buzzer. A steward in a short white jacket came in and was given the order. The big man, who had the aspect of an admiral who didn't like being in a shore job, got to his feet and strode up and down the room, hands clasped behind his back. The coffee came quickly; and three minutes after its arrival the red telephone rang. The big man grabbed it up. 'Yes? Yes, Prime Minister.' He stared expressionlessly across the room, eyes fixed on Freeman without seeing him. It was a short conversation. When the call was cut from the other end the big man banged the receiver down and said, 'You could almost smell the cigar smoke down the line. *And* the fire and brimstone.'

'Angry?'

'Wouldn't you be if you were him? A pet scheme gone adrift. Someone's balls are going to be had for breakfast, I can tell you. Not the poor bloody men on the spot – Intelligence, not *us*, the RAF side, the recce boys. And whoever had too big a mouth, if there's been a leak from this side of the Channel.'

'And in the meantime, sir?'

There was a chilly grin, more like a grimace. 'If the old man has his way, it'll be all stops pulled out. But he'll meet opposition from the service chiefs. Even he can't upset the overall strategy of the war.'

'You mean they may be left to it, sir?'

'That's just what I mean. Sometimes we're all bastards, Freeman.'

Away across the West End, deep in the war room strongpoint built underground not far from the Houses of Parliament, a bulky figure, also in dressing-gown and pyjamas, was hunched over a cigar with his head between his hands. Standing before him was the First Sea Lord, who had been having a hard time for the last few minutes. Patiently he had advanced his arguments: it was a nasty business to leave the two remaining ships to it, of course it was. But the ships of the Navy were so widely scattered, escorts could not be withdrawn from any of the convoys currently at sea, that was obvious, and the availability of ships in port was, frankly, very little indeed. So many were undergoing badly needed refits, others were boiler-cleaning and thus also out of the war for the time being . . .

'Can't you find a damn battleship, for God's sake?'

'Possibly, sir, but for what purpose?'

'Bombard Brest, of course! Fifteen-inch guns . . .'

'Think of the French, sir – '

There was an angry snap. 'I've been thinking of the French ever since Dunkirk. Do you imagine that de Gaulle has allowed me to forget them for one moment, First Sea Lord?'

'I take your point, sir. But remember the whole point of

105

Scatter was to keep French casualties to a minimum. It still has to be an inside job, sir.'

'Oh, don't talk to me like a detective sergeant, First Sea Lord.' There was an angry wave of the cigar. 'The bombardment at this stage would be no more than simple assistance to our own men – '

'I disagree, Prime Minister. I suggest that it would be little more than revenge since it won't be useful – '

'What's wrong with revenge, may I ask?'

'For one thing it'll kill more Frenchmen than Germans. The military presence is considerably less than the French civilian population. It'll cause enormous resentment, sir. And you'll have a strong reaction from General de Gaulle – '

'Bugger General de Gaulle.'

'Yes, sir. But neither he nor ourselves wanted civilian casualties.'

'Not so long as they could be avoided – that's the nub. If they *can't* damn well be avoided – '

'Yes, sir,' the First Sea Lord said again. 'But I repeat, the preservation of the French and of their goodwill has been of prime and basic importance – '

'Never mind all that! I insist upon succouring those poor fellows in the *Rard* of Brest, whatever *Rard* might mean.' The Prime Minister still refused to pronounce French properly, spoke it with a sneer, as one way of getting back at General de Gaulle. 'Now, kindly see that my insistence is acted upon promptly. If you don't want to use a battleship, find something else effective, but don't delay.'

It was a partial climb-down and the First Sea Lord, whose own desire was in fact to do exactly what the Prime Minister wanted but knew he couldn't, had to be content with it. Orders, after a paper survey of the Naval dockyards and the ships in them had been made, went to the Commander-in-Chief Home Fleet in Scapa: a heavy cruiser was to be squeezed out of his operational area and sent with all despatch towards Brest, where she was to lie off at a distance and await orders. There was a difficulty insofar as the senior officer of Operation Scatter could not be contacted other than in plain language; a contingency in which coded or cyphered contact might need to be made had not been envisaged, or if it had it had been negatived in the larger interest of preserving the security of the Naval communications system. Before long, however, someone dreamed up the idea of transmitting an innocuous-sounding PL message that would serve to let the senior officer know that he had not been forgotten and that help was on the way.

The result of this reached Cameron via Petty Officer Telegraphist Gander a couple of hours after the German aircraft had once again flown away and left them in peace – the peace of a heavy snowstorm that had answered Archer's prayer in double quick time. The ships were covered; whitened, they made their slow onward progress towards the anchorage with Terry-Jones sending back the soundings by his shaded battery Aldis. But soon the snow became too thick; with the visibility down to nil – even the fo'c'sle was barely visible beyond Number Two gun – Cameron gave the order to heave-to and the whaler was recalled by use of a megaphone.

It was as the whaler scraped alongside that Gander reported to the forebridge. 'Signal, sir. Addressed Scatter. Just that, no call sign.'

'Signal, for God's sake! Who the hell from, Gander?'

'No originator shown, sir. Funny message an' all. Short. Reads, *Proverbs one thirty-three*. In plain language.'

'That's all?

'Yes, sir. Time of origin, 0735 GMT, sir.'

Cameron met Archer's eye. Archer said, 'Bible.'

'That's what I was thinking, Number One. Anybody got one?'

'I'll check round, sir. If there was, it could have gone overboard.'

'Let's hope not.' Archer went down the ladder; even the treads of the ladders were thick with snow, freezing where seaboots had trodden the stuff flat. A pipe was made: Anyone Possessing a Bible to Report to the Bridge. Leading Seaman

McNee reported from the director that he had one on his person. He wasn't going to be parted from it so he'd shoved it in the pocket of his duffel-coat. There was no reprimand from the skipper for orders disobeyed. McNee clambered down from the director and handed the Bible to Cameron, who read out Proverbs chapter one, verse 33.

'But whoso hearkeneth unto me shall dwell safely, and shall be quiet from fear of evil.' He closed the Bible. He said, 'Addressed Scatter, which shouldn't convey anything to the Nazis. It looks as though we have a friend somewhere out at sea, Number One. Pass the word below, will you? We're not on our own any more. But tell 'em not to go mad about it. We don't want sounds to spread to the evil-minded.' He added, 'We'd better tell *Probity*.'

Gander said, 'She'll have picked the signal up too, sir.'

'They may not have a Bible,' Cameron said. He handed McNee's property back, with thanks. McNee climbed up to the director again and showed the officer the relevant passage.

Midshipman Richards said with a grin, 'There's times when Bible bashers come up with the goods, all right!'

'It's not that,' McNee said with a touch of huffiness.

'It's not?'

'No. It's direct contact.'

Richards looked blank. He got an earful thereafter. McNee had seen the hand of God. It was going to be all right now; the signal wasn't going to be hauled close up. Not yet, not this trip. Midshipman Richards was glad to hear it; but there was a lot of war yet to be fought. He was left with the impression that Leading Seaman McNee didn't for one moment believe that the w/T message had come from any earthly helping hand.

The snowstorm continued. By now there was little of the ship to be seen except around the funnel casing and the funnels themselves sticking up like grey ghosts, disembodied things attached to nothing but the snow itself. In the almost silent engine-room Chief ERA Osgood was on edge, wondering if all his hands, many of whom were out of his line of sight, were loafing about, taking the opportunity provided by the lack of anything to do – which was how they would think of it. In Osgood's view there never was a time in any engine-room when there was nothing to do. Polishing, wiping around with a handful of cotton waste, greasing bearings – oh, there was never a spare moment.

He wished he could leave the starting platform for a prowl, but now was not the time for that. The bridge might want his engines at any moment, literally. A matter of life and death with all those Jerries around.

Osgood yawned. He'd been yawning the last couple of hours.

Talk about dead tired! He'd been on the go now, on his feet on the starting platform, for what – more than twelve hours. Twelve hours . . . a long time in its own right yet it seemed like a whole lifetime since the ships had cleared from Barry docks with the convoy. And there wasn't going to be any respite yet. Osgood yawned again, his mouth seemed to stretch open and stay there as if it wasn't ever going to close again. He leaned back against the steel bulkhead, arms folded across his chest, and a moment later fell asleep standing up. ERA Hoskin, coming towards the starting platform a few minutes later, wiping oily hands on his overalls, saw the sleeping Chief and clicked his tongue sardonically.

'Court martial offence, is that,' he said in a loud voice.

Osgood came awake and almost fell over. 'What's that, Hoskin?'

'Going to sleep on watch.'

'I never! Bloody cheek.' Osgood waved his arms angrily; just then the telegraph bells rang and the pointers went to Slow Ahead and the engine-room came back to life. Then the bridge came on the phone, the Captain speaking. The snow was easing, the visibility was good enough and he was proceeding to the inshore anchorage. He was going with the flood tide and there should be a safe margin to clear the mudbanks.

The snow, very widespread over the whole Brest area, had swept south of the British ships and had brought its white blanket to Port Launay where Henri Chalandon was agitating himself about his unwelcome guests, who were fast asleep. When they woke from their exhaustion, both physical and mental no doubt, all the emotion of Marcel's death would be visited upon him and he would be obliged to sound sympathetic and provide comfort. Grieving persons Henri found tiresome, there was so much they wanted and no will to get it for themselves. Brandy . . . Henri's eyes glittered with foreboding. Brandy he had, but wasn't going to say so. There was red wine, cheap enough, and that would have to do. As Henri Chalandon sat warming himself before a fire, and glaring out at the appalling snow which was going to make funerals difficult if it went on and on as sometimes it did – as he sat there wearing his black beret and a thick, drab-coloured jersey so as to add to the fire's warmth and save coal, the Gestapo came. There was a thunderous knock at the cottage door and when Henri Chalandon opened it there they were, black uniforms and caps with shiny peaks and a profusion of weapons, the officer wearing steel-rimmed spectacles that gave some sort of shape to a face devoid of eyebrows. Chalandon knew him: Hauptmann Schmelcher, local Gestapo chief.

'Herr Hauptmann Schmelcher . . . *bonjour, m'sieur.*'

Schmelcher put a foot in the doorway and shouldered his way in, followed by his men. 'It is a filthy morning to stand about,' he said in good French. 'You have had visitors. I wish to see them.'

'My brother's – '

'We know about your brother. Word was telephoned from Brest. In Brest there was trouble.' Schmelcher saw no reason to go into details. The facts had been made known to him clearly. From an upstairs window in the outskirts of Brest a man of Vichy had seen shooting and had recognized under-taker Duhamel and had very properly reported it. Duhamel's home, which was also his place of business, had been visited

110

immediately and Mme Duhamel had been dragged from her bed. There had been some screaming and then she had talked. A messy business, Brest had reported, and a lot of blood, but before Madame Duhamel had died she had spoken the name of the corpse: Marcel Chalandon.

Henri said, 'My sister-in-law and niece, they are asleep – '

'You will wake them at once.'

Henri shrugged; the Gestapo must at all costs be kept in with, they were all-powerful and they ruled France. Charles de Gaulle was a traitor, bringing fratricide to the French people. He should have accepted the inevitable, then there would have been no suspicions about who in France was for him and who was not. Grumbling about all this and about the monster Churchill who was using the French to his own advantage, Henri Chalandon, with a gun in his back, led the way up the narrow, ricketty stairs and knocked on the door of his sister-in-law's bedroom. There was no reply and the door was locked from the inside. Hauptmann Schmelcher put his boot against it and kicked it in.

The room was empty.

Schmelcher's voice was like ice. 'The other woman?'

It was the same again. Both gone. 'The undertakers?'

Henri Chalandon said, 'A room in the village. At the inn.'

There was only the one inn. Hauptmann Schmelcher went there in person, with two of his squad. The third man remained with Chalandon, keeping him covered with his automatic rifle. It was not long before Schmelcher was back, angrier than ever but still icy. The browless eyes stared through the steel rims at Henri Chalandon. The face was almost as pale as the snow outside.

'Gone. Now the corpse. And after that . . .' He left the rest unsaid. Chalandon took him out to the back of the cottage, where the hearse still stood. The coffin was dragged out and smashed open and brother Marcel was tipped onto the bare earth and stripped of his shroud. Schmelcher stared down at the corpse and gave it a kick. 'A traitor,' he said. 'Of the *maquis*.'

111

'*Mais non!*' Henri was genuinely shaken.

'Yes.' Schmelcher gestured at his squad and they advanced on the hearse. They took it apart, prising metal and woodwork with the barrels of their rifles, tearing, ripping. Henri had no idea what they expected to find, but they didn't appear to have found it. Furious now, Hauptmann Schmelcher propelled Henri back against the wall of his cottage and then took him across the face, right and left repeatedly, with his revolver barrel until the face was a bloody pulp and Henri Chalandon fell moaning to the ground beside the desecrated corpse of his brother. He was not permitted to lie there; hands dragged him to his feet and he was frog-marched away, sobbing. *Sacré Dieu*, what a terrible catastrophe . . . he said over and over again that he was loyal to Marshal Pétain, a good Vichy man who wanted no trouble. If his brother had been a traitor that was not his fault. They took no notice of him. He felt utter despair. Perhaps this was why Marcel had joined the Resistance, joined it because of men like these? But the mad dog Churchill would be worse – always and always the Germans were saying so on the wireless, so was the Vichy government. Churchill interrogated prisoners personally and burned them cruelly with his cigars, frothing at the mouth as he did so, and he had infected all the British forces and police with his poison. In Britain there was a terrible organization called the Home Guard, filled with unprincipled men released from the prisons by order of Churchill to enforce his rule, men who were much worse than the Gestapo.

Nevertheless, knowing he was in for it whether or not the Gestapo were angels in disguise, Henri Chalandon took his chance when it came. One of the men holding him slipped on a patch of ice and went headlong, dragging Chalandon down with him in so forceful a manner that the other guard was dragged down too. In the mêlée, in which the first man broke his leg, Chalandon found himself free of any grip and without thought for the consequences he ran for it. He had gone no more than a dozen metres when the guns opened and his colandered body, falling, twitched for a while and then lay still and silent in the blood-stained snow.

From the back of a cottage fronting the quay, the address being one that old Marcel Chalandon had often quoted as a safe house occupied by a man and woman of the Resistance, Marie and her mother watched, concealed behind the slats of the shutters. Marie, who in fact had not slept at all, had seen the Gestapo's approach earlier from Uncle Henri's window and had woken her mother just in time as the Boche had slipped and slithered on their way. It was no more than instinct, really, that had told her the Gestapo were intending to visit her uncle's house – that, and her knowledge of her own involvement in certain affairs. The drop from the bedroom window to the roof of the hearse had not been a long one and quickly she had knotted blankets together to form a lowering rope for her mother. The two women had reached the back garden just as the loud knocking had come, and the knocking itself, so boastful, so loudly demanding in the name of the hateful Führer, had itself helped to conceal any other sounds.

They had reached the bottom of the garden before Schmelcher had forced his way into the cottage. Wearing their night clothes and some of Uncle Henri's blankets, they had made their way to the safe house where they had been welcomed as Marcel Chalandon's family. As now the Gestapo marched away, one of the men dragging Uncle Henri's bleeding body behind him like a dead sheep, by one leg, the women went down the stairs to breakfast and a blazing fire. There was no appetite but the kindly woman of the house persuaded Marie at least to fill her stomach a little. Some ten minutes later the woman's husband, who had left the cottage soon after the Chalandons had arrived, returned with extraordinary news.

'A man has come into the village,' he said, keeping his voice low in case the Gestapo had ears even inside his home. 'He has come in his fishing boat from beyond Landevennec at the entry to the Aulne. There was as much snow there as has been here . . . but when it began to clear, this man saw two

113

warships.'

'Warships?'

'Yes. He believes them to be British. Once he served in our Navy, and sometimes he met British ships. These, he said, were of an old class of British destroyers.' The man paused. 'You spoke earlier of things that happened in Brest. There is a connection, yes?'

Marie nodded and went to her mother and laid her hands on her shoulders. To the man of the house she said, 'Yes, I believe the ships may be British. We – ' She checked. Whoever you were talking to in France there was an overriding need for discretion and not to talk too much to those who might be tortured by the Gestapo. 'No chances' was the watchword in a sad country. She said, 'That is where I wish to go, to England. That is where I *will* go, with my mother, if we can be got there. I wish to take my mother to England, *m'sieur*. I wish this very much. I have had enough of fighting and worrying and seeing so many good people die. I have had enough.'

Then she broke down and wept, for her dead father and for France.

11

The whaler was in the water again and the soundings were being continually reported back by Terry-Jones. *Palatine* and *Probity* moved on dead slow with only just enough water beneath them at times: it was touch and go. Or rather, Cameron thought, touch and never go again if they bit deep enough into the mud. His nerves were on edge now; he wanted to reach some sort of cover, some sort of shelter, before the Germans came in again. He wanted to cram on speed but couldn't. He had discussed plans with Archer: his intention was to leave the destroyers at anchor and get all members of both ships' companies ashore and then let the German aircraft waste their bombs and canon fire on deserted ships that were in any case doomed never to leave the Rade de Brest.

'Then what do we do?'

'Get back to Brest, Number One. Hide up when necessary but make all the speed we can when we're in the clear. Then act as soldiers and make contact with what's left of the commandos.'

'Are you still going to try to blow up the U-boat shelters, sir?'

'If we can, we will. That's all I can say – '

'How?' Archer asked pointedly.

Cameron said, 'I've no idea in the world, Number One. What I'm doing is all we can do now. Join up with the commandos and all get out together – '

'We'll never make it. Not a hope.'

'We'll still make the attempt. My idea was, to try to reach the coast north of Brest and look for a boat. Either some fisherman that wants to get out himself, or we nick one. But that situation's changed now, changed for the better.'

'That w/t message?'

Cameron nodded. 'Yes. We've a good chance of being picked up, either from a remote part of the coast or at sea. Once we rejoin the commandos, we'll be able to make contact by radio so long as the ship that sent the message isn't out of range.'

'And if the commandos' transmitter's been shot up, or captured?'

Cameron said patiently, 'If we stopped to think of all the things that might or might not have happened, Number One, we might just as well stop engines here and now and wait for the bloody Huns to come and bomb us to kingdom come. All right?'

Archer flushed. His tone was stiff when he said, 'It's my job, I would have thought, to anticipate difficulties.'

'True enough. But not to be a determined pessimist.'

The First Lieutenant made no response to that. He saluted and turned away down the ladder, face still flushed. The RNVR was too bloody big for its boots and he believed Cameron had handled everything wrong from the start. It had to be admitted that they might well have been sunk if they'd tried to fight their way out through the Goulet, but at least they'd have stood some sort of chance of making the open sea, and as for the commandos, Archer didn't believe for a moment they were likely to find any alive and free. At any rate a commanding officer could hardly be blamed for making the assumption they were all dead or in the bag, and his first duty, in Archer's view, was to his own ship and his own men. There were times in this life and in this war when you had to take the main chance and think about yourself. The commandos had known well enough what they were in for, and neither Shawcross nor his colour-sergeant nor any of the marines would expect the Navy to pull their chestnuts out of the fire

116

for them. The Navy's part had been done when they'd been landed, and if they didn't come back to be re-embarked, well, it was no skin off the Navy's nose and no one could say it was. Walking aft along the upper deck, Archer knew he could have said all this to Cameron, but he hadn't, and he knew himself why he hadn't: it wasn't really strict Naval reasoning to say the fate of the commandos didn't matter and he had recalled once again the attitude years ago of the commander of the Mediterranean Fleet flagship. Cameron's reaction would probably have been similar. He was that sort of person: an overdeveloped sense of duty and obligation. All right up to a point; Archer believed they had passed that point the moment Cameron had taken the ships south into the Rade. But it was too late now. There was even a chance that Cameron was right, here and now in the situation they had been dropped into, to think about abandoning, to try to get out without a ship that had become an encumbrance. It had been done before, singly if not in an unwieldy great group of seamen and *maquis* – the men who had escaped from the German POW camps and made their way south, down to Spain and Gibraltar and home. But they hadn't any bees in their bonnets about blowing up U-boat shelters on the way. That was really what stuck in Archer's throat, he realized.

Cameron wouldn't be able to do it anyway and afterwards he was damned if he wouldn't say I told you so.

A prey to his restless thoughts and apprehensions Archer turned for'ard again. He'd been walking aft aimlessly, but First Lieutenants always had roving commissions and it wouldn't have shown.

But it had.

Mr Cantley, observing the First Lieutenant's pre-occupied look, sniffed and wiped the back of his hand across his nose. Jimmy, he reflected, wasn't showing up the RN in a very good light. Jimmy wasn't the sort who liked to get his hands dirty, for one thing. In the opinion of Mr Cantley, experienced in summing up men fast, he was more of the socialite Naval officer than a seaman. He'd have done fine aboard a

117

battleship or cruiser in pre-war days, swanning around the Med or the home ports or sampling the high life in Hong Kong or Singapore. He wasn't possible to imagine taking charge when something unexpected went wrong. Cantley didn't think he was a coward – not that; but he would be caught badly on the hop in an emergency that he hadn't encountered before, it being precisely under such conditions that the real basic seaman instinct tended to emerge in a man if it was there. Fair-weather sailor, that was Jimmy the One. But of course it took all sorts and you got bad Jimmies the same as you got bad quacks and bad plumbers. While it lasted it had to be borne stoically, but Cantley hoped Archer was going to come through all this without panicking at a bad moment.

As the First Lieutenant made his way for'ard he was hailed from the bridge. 'About to anchor, Number One.'

Archer acknowledged and climbed the ladder to the fo'c'sle. Special Sea Dutymen were piped. The skies had cleared to some extent now, the snow had stopped for the time being and the horizons were more distant. On the forebridge Cameron, bent to the azimuth circle on the gyro repeater, watched his leading marks for the anchorage. For some while now, ever since clearing the entry to the Rade, the starboard anchor, now the only one remaining, had been veered to the waterline, ready for letting go in an emergency. With the slips now knocked away, Archer was in his position in the eyes of the ship, green anchor flag ready in his hand. As the bearings came on Cameron raised his own twin of the anchor flag; Archer did likewise. At the centre-line capstan, the shipwright stood by to let go the brake.

Cameron dropped his flag in a rapid motion and called out, '*Let go!*'

Archer's flag came down, the shipwright released the brake on which the anchor was riding, and the cable ran out in a cloud of red dust, to be brought up at three shackles. It seemed to tense ears to make a thunderous noise, enough to wake the dead. As Archer, leaning over the starboard guardrail, watched the cable markings and then lifted his

118

hand to check the outrush, there was a shout from the forebridge, the voice of Yeoman of Signals Leckwith.

'On the shore, sir! Green three-oh. Looks like Frenchies waving to us, sir.'

Earlier, as the snow that had stopped falling on Port Launay came back again, Marie Chalandon and her mother had been taken to the quay where the fisherman who had brought word of the British warships was waiting for them. The fisherman, Pierre Guichard, was a Gaullist and a member of the *maquis*, and, contacted by the man from the safe house, had readily agreed to take the two women to where the British ships had been seen, at the same time giving a warning that they might not still be where he had seen them – on the other hand, they had had the look of ships seeking an anchorage and it was very possible they had eventually anchored inside the river mouth off Landevennec. There should be enough water there. He pointed out the dangers: to embark aboard a British ship trapped in the Rade was, to say the least, crazy. But Marie had been adamant. Already they were in danger enough and the only way out of it would be via the British Navy, who must surely have support outside the Goulet. Marie was ready for any danger now, having seen what had happened to Uncle Henri. So Pierre Guichard had shrugged and said he was willing. He made arrangements for the party to embark and the attention of the Nazi patrol set to watch the boats was engaged by the firing of a pistol from a brave *maquisard* in another of the fishing-boats made fast to the quay some distance from Guichard's boat. The women boarded at a moment when by great good luck the snow happened to start falling very thickly again; they were conveyed through the snowstorm in two handcarts loaded with fish baskets. Guichard lost not time in getting under way thereafter, thrusting his boat from the quay by powerful shoves of the boathooks and then gliding out with the use of oars until it was safe to start his engine, which then chugged defiance back towards Port Launay and Hauptmann Schmelcher. When

Schmelcher's search of the cottages ended in dismal failure and the stopping of the snow revealed the absence of Guichard's boat his fury knew no bounds; but when it had subsided he was able to see a brighter side: if the wretched Gaullists had got out from under his nose by means of the fishing-boat, then it was possible they might lead him to other Gaullist fish.

With his men, he got into his military transport and motored towards Landevennec after first telephoning through to Chateaulin in case the boat had headed up river.

'The Gaullists,' he said to his second-in-command, 'are now trapped. They will not get away again.' It was a satisfactory thought and he had no doubts that it would be he himself who would make the capture. Already he had been warned by telephone of the presence of enemy warships in the Rade; clearly the Gaullists had some connection with that and they would be heading to make contact. Schmelcher smiled to himself: it was impossible to fool the Gestapo! He grew impatient when the lying snow impeded the progress of his truck in spite of tyre chains and he had to use the spades with his men. Impatience quickly became anger: snow could not be allowed to impede the Third Reich. But it did. Hauptmann Schmelcher found himself very seriously delayed and in the end was obliged to continue his journey on foot, lifting one jackboot after another in his Führer's interest and occasionally falling flat into deep snow.

Marie alias Clémentine and her mother had beaten Schmelcher to it after an anxious river trip. Put ashore before the fishing-boat reached the end of the cover provided by steep, wooded hills on both sides of the river, they headed overland for some half a mile towards the waters of the Rade. They saw the British ships with intense relief and began waving and calling out. Octavius, on the bridge of *Palatine* with Cameron, had snatched up a pair of binoculars when the yeoman of signals had reported.

'It is Clémentine, *m'sieur*!' he said with much excitement.

'The girl at the barracks – '

'*Oui, m'sieur.*'

Cameron called down to the fo'c'sle, 'Number One, the whaler. Inshore at once, fast as they can make it.'

'Aye, aye, sir.' In the whaler, Terry-Jones had heard the Captain's order. Quickly he got the boat on course for the waving group on the shore. The ratings pulled strongly: there was a look of desperation about the women, as though they were only one jump ahead of pursuit, and no one was going to see them taken by the Nazis or the Vichy French. Terry-Jones had been an OD in the battleship *Valiant* when Admiral Somerville had been forced reluctantly to open fire on the French fleet in Mers-el-Kebir on 3 July 1940 and had watched in horror as the British projectiles had sunk the *Bretagne*, while the *Dunkerque* and *Provence* had been seriously damaged with heavy loss of life to the French ships' companies. To have been forced by action of Darlan and Pétain to take part in something like that had rankled. In some ways the Vichy French were worse than Hitler . . . Terry-Jones brought the whaler into the shallows, touching lightly on a muddy bottom, hauling off again a little so that the extra weight to be embarked shouldn't put him down to stick fast. They came aboard, the old mother being assisted by the boat's crew and looking as though she'd had quite enough of war. They were aboard when Terry-Jones heard aircraft engines in the distance and saw the British HA guns already swinging round to bear. He made the decision to remain inshore and hope his human cargo could be kept out of the battle.

Aboard *Palatine* the ack-ack gunners had a slice of luck as the bombers came in. A shell burst immediately in front of the leading aircraft, which blew up in a burst of flame and smoke, and twisted down to take the water some way north of the destroyers. Three more swept in, coming low to rake the decks with cannon fire. Petty Officer Lunt, the quarterdeck division PO, took a shell in his back and disintegrated. In the director Richards had a very close shave for the second time since leaving Barry so short a time before. Beside him

121

Leading Seaman McNee sagged in his seat, his face a mask of blood and drooling brains.

'Poor bugger,' Richards said aloud, feeling the shake in his fingers. He wondered – having had that ear-bashing earlier – where McNee had gone, wondered if he was already climbing through the Birks of Aberfeldy. But wherever his spirit was, his earthly body was very present and causing an obstruction. Richards eased it away as best he could and carried on with the war single-handed. At the guns there had been more casualties and on the bridge Yeoman of Signals Leckwith had had an arm shattered and was awaiting attention by the Surgeon Lieutenant, bleeding like a pig in the meantime. Stripey Trudge, thinking of his premonition, the one brought on by his ponderings on his dad in the last lot, had sustained a flesh wound in his backside and was half convinced he was dead already or anyway on his way – the wound was bloody painful and his medical knowledge was nil. It could be fatal for all he knew.

The three aircraft swung away and climbed for what looked as if it was going to be a bombing run and was. One of them was caught by the umbrella of flak and followed the earlier one, blowing up and dropping in bits and pieces into the water before it could drop any of its bomb-load.

The remaining two dropped their sticks.

Many of the bombs went into the water not far off *Probity*. There were great spouts of water and spray fell on *Probity*, obscuring her outline in ton upon ton of upflung sea. Then *Palatine* took her death blow: a bomb came down smack at the base of the fore funnel and penetrated to explode in the boiler-room, deep inside the ship, a massive, tamped explosion. The boiler-room, the boilers, all the stokers, were fragmented immediately, and the raging of burning oil-fuel was added to the explosion itself. In the engine-room Chief ERA Osgood was aware of his enclosed kingdom glowing red-hot and the ladders melting in the instant before he died in a sheet of flame. The explosion blasted through to the upper deck. In the wardroom Surgeon Lieutenant Pratt died as he was handling a scalpel; LSBA Cleek died whilst bandaging a badly shattered thigh. All along the decks men went flat; waves of demoniac heat blasted fore and aft, singeing hair, causing burns. Desperately Archer was shouting for the fire parties and the damage control parties; but it was already much too late. He ran for the bridge ladder.

Cameron asked, 'Well?'

'We've had it. Fires can't be brought under control, not a hope in hell. Anyway the bottom's blown out of her.'

Cameron looked along his burning decks, looked at total chaos, at blood and mangled, burning bodies. He felt dead inside, blaming himself now for entering the Rade on a fool's errand. 'What a bloody muck-up,' he said savagely.

'What do we do?' Archer asked.

'All we *can* do now. Abandon ship.'

'Aye, aye, sir.' Archer turned and shouted the order fore and aft from the forebridge. It was repeated by Chief Petty Officer King, who had come out from the wheelhouse and was looking appalled at what he saw. King moved about the shattered decks and superstructure, encouraging with his presence, giving a helping hand to the wounded who would have to be taken across to *Probity*. *Probity* appeared to have escaped intact, at least structurally. But she too had been strafed by cannon fire; and obviously the Jerries, who had drawn off for now, would be back before long.

Cameron took up the loud hailer and tried the switch: no use, as he'd expected. He used a megaphone and called across to the whaler.

'Pick up all the men you can, then make alongside *Probity*, Terry-Jones! We're settling, main deck awash.'

The sub acknowledged with a wave. Alongside him Marie was looking white and scared, her mother was crying, shaking all over and fingering a rosary. The whaler's crew pulled fast to pick up survivors as men went over the side all along *Palatine*'s length. There was only one Carley float left intact for the use of the wounded; but *Probity*'s whaler was coming across now. Stripey Trudge hung about the slanted deck, close to the Carley float, looking anxious and clasping, with difficulty, his rear end.

'What's up, Trudge?' This was the gunner's mate, his oilskin running blood. 'Waiting for a lift, are you, by any chance?'

'Wounded, GI,' Stripey said promptly. 'Walking wounded, like.'

'Swimming wounded an' all,' Todd said. 'Get on with you, you fat lump o' lard!'

'I can't, GI, I – '

'No such bloody word as can't, Able Seaman Trudge. Bugger off an' don't expect to take up the room of men that's a bloody sight worse off than what you are, all right?'

'Filthy dirty Frog water – '

'And don't bloody argue,' Todd snapped, losing his temper. 'Water's good for wounds, washes 'em, see? So shove your bum in it before I kick you over the side.'

Muttering and looking vicious, Stripey moved aft where, thanks to the slant, he could slide in rather than jump, which might be bad for his arse. He cursed again as the water stung and he visualized all the horrible French germs swimming around in it. It would probably turn gangrenous and rot away for all the GI cared, the sod. Trudge swam slowly away using a ponderous breast-stroke and looking like a porpoise with a sou'-wester on its head.

Cameron left the bridge after all hands had gone, Leckwith and others badly wounded strapped into Neil Robinson stretchers. He went over the side quickly, no backward looks for a lost command, but with a heart like lead. The Resistance man, Octavius, tried to comfort him.

'France will be grateful, *m'sieur*. We shall remember the sacrifice.'

'They may be grateful to the men. Not to me.'

'But *m'sieur* – '

'All right. No need to say any more, *m'sieur*. You've lost men too today.' It was only too true: many of the bodies left behind were French. Octavius himself, before saying he was ready to leave the ship, had himself gone round all the dead Frenchmen and removed anything that might identify them to the detriment, when the Germans came aboard, of their families. He had wanted to remove the bodies in case of facial recognition but had seen that this was not a practical possibility. He had compromised with his conscience by lifting them and dragging them to *Palatine*'s side and dropping them into the water. It was the best that could be done.

A sad band of survivors was brought aboard *Probity* to be welcomed by her First Lieutenant, an RNVR named Harrison. Cameron enquired about her Captain.

'Still in a coma, sir. Worse if anything. The doctor hasn't much hope, but he hasn't been written off yet.'

'You've taken over command of your ship?' Cameron asked.

'Yes. What's the position now?'

Cameron said, 'You remain in command of *Probity*, of course. I'm still in the role of senior officer of the group as a result of Farnon's death and your captain being on the sick list.'

'Yes, that's understood, sir.' Harrison paused. 'Orders, sir?'

Cameron said heavily, 'We stand by for further attack, for a start. In the meantime we'll have a council of war – if that isn't too grandiose a term for what's left of us!'

The Germans didn't come back, leaving an uneasy truce hanging over the south-eastern segment of the Rade. Soon after Cameron had climbed to *Probity*'s bridge the Petty Officer Telegraphist reported a lot of confusion picked up on the local Port Wave.

'What sort of confusion?' Cameron asked.

'Chatter, sir. In Frog lingo and what I reckon is German. Like a load of monkeys. Hysterical, that might be the word. Then they went right off the air, very sudden.'

Cameron nodded thoughtfully. 'What's your estimate, PO?'

'Jerries in a panic about something, sir. Now, that might

125

mean they're under attack up in Brest, but I dunno – might mean anything, I s'pose, sir.'

Cameron said, 'We don't want to be too optimistic and I'd have thought we would have heard something of an attack. On the other hand, the airfield north of Brest could be out of hearing from here.' He paced the bridge for a while then turned to Harrison. He said, 'that signal . . .'

'The biblical reference?'

'Yes. That has to mean the home authorities are doing something. They could have made their tiny minds up at last to act positively and bomb the airfields. In which case – and this is probably too much to hope for – those four aircraft were the ones that got away. The only ones operational in the vicinity, the only ones immediately available anyway. It won't last, but it may give us time.'

Harrison asked, 'Time for what?'

'Time will tell,' Cameron said with a faint grin. All was not lost yet. 'We'll have that council of war right away. We've still got one ship left and we're going to do our best to secure the original objective – and then get out to sea.' He said that with more hope than belief.

The word was passed for all officers to muster on the bridge immediately. So far as *Palatine* was concerned there was a full muster apart from Burton and the Surgeon Lieutenant. *Probity* had lost four of her officers as well as some thirty ratings. Between them the two ships had had a strong force of the Resistance aboard but of these many had been killed in the air attacks, mostly aboard *Probity*. They still had forty plus what was left of the ships' companies. When the word came down for the bridge muster, Mr Cantley, lucky to be alive and knowing it, was having a word amidships with his gunner's mate.

'Fish, Jack,' he said, smacking the palm of his hand against one of the starboard-side torpedo tubes. 'They never took the buggers out of *Probity* like they did us.'

'Wonder why.'

'No accounting for the whims of the Admiralty,' Cantley

said briskly, 'though I do remember *Palatine* was said to have had some trouble back in thirty-nine . . . probably cheaper and quicker to take out the tubes from an old tub – but I don't know and I'm not worried. Thing is, they've given me an idea.'

Todd met his eye. 'Use the fish, sir?'

'Yes, why not? Against those U-boat pens. Skipper had some notion he could use the depth charges. Barmy, that. But fish, now! You just got to get into position, and wham!'

'Suggest it to the skipper, then?'

'That's the ticket.' Cantley paused. 'Trouble is, I've been told *Probity*'s lost her gunner (T) and her TI. Know anything about fish, do you?'

'Not a lot, sir. You?'

'Smattering . . .'

'How about an LTO?' Todd asked, in reference to the non-substantive rate of leading torpedoman.

Cantley nodded. 'Bloke called Ledger – I'll be having a word with him. Hang on for orders, Jack.' Cantley went to the bridge. He found Cameron sketching out his ideas for a landing closer to the port of Brest. They had, Cameron said, a reasonably well-armed force. They could also, he said, count on the Resistance in Brest plus any of the commandos that could be contacted. The question of explosives for use against the shelters, however, remained.

Cantley said, 'I reckon we can cope, sir.'

'How's that, Guns?'

Cantley put forward his ideas. He added, 'Neither the GI nor me are experts on fish, sir, but I reckon we can manage with the help of *Probity*'s LTO.'

Cameron was dubious. Torpedoes could cause a certain amount of havoc, it was true, at any rate to the exterior of the base – if they could be aimed spot on through the entry. Cantley said that in his opinion enough fish would do more than cause external damage, they would penetrate and bugger up the whole complex. Cameron glanced at Octavius and asked, 'What do you think, *m'sieur*? Is there a clear

127

approach to the actual entry to the shelters?'

Octavius said there was. If the ship steamed back across the Rade and re-entered the port area between Isle Longue and Pointe de l'Armorique, and then swung to starboard into the northern arm of the Rade, she would steam past the entry channel used by the U-boats. In theory at any rate, since the outer caissons and gates had not yet been completed, it might be possible to fire torpedoes straight into the middle of the construction work.

There had to be a snag, of course. Cameron didn't need to ask what it was: the moment he put *Probity*'s bows into the Goulet everything in the port of Brest would open on him. The U-boats' entry point was some distance along the northern arm, Octavius said, and to reach it would be a much more tricky matter than the original approach to the inner harbour for the landing of the commandos. Much luck would be needed – the chances of getting through would be slim. Cameron weighed a whole set of imponderables in his mind. He had to do something now: at any moment the German air attacks could be resumed and they could be blown out of the water here in the Rade. Those thoughts about renewed British bombing had been no more than conjecture, even wishful thinking which was always dangerous.

He spoke to Cantley. 'I don't know, Guns. It could work out but I can't rely on it a hundred per cent. There has to be something else as well.'

'Such as what, sir?'

'I don't know yet . . . the lines I'm thinking along are, if we can get a shore party into the eastern part of Brest, and muster *maquis* support, then we could mount a diversion in the port itself.'

'With the ship heading back north and standing by for a torpedo attack?' Harrison asked.

'Something like that. If it's to succeed, we've just got to draw off the Germans for long enough to make the entry to the pens. It'll be touch and go. But we just might pull it off, I suppose.' He turned to Cantley. 'Guns, you and the GI had

better cut along and pick the LTO's brains. No decisions yet
. . . there'll be further orders when I've worked things out
with Lieutenant Harrison.'

'Aye, aye, sir.' Cantley went down the ladder, collected the
gunner's mate and sent word for Leading Seaman Ledger to
report amidships on the iron deck. Ledger got the word while
he was drinking a cup of kye in the galley: Ledger, a three-
badgeman of much experience of the ways of the Andrew,
knew precisely when he could snatch a moment of ease
without being accused of absence from duty, and now, while
the officers were nattering on the bridge and no doubt coming
to sod-all conclusions, was as good a time as any.

'Who's this Cantley?' he asked the messenger.

'Gunner of *Palatine*, Killick.'

'Tell 'im to stuff 'imself,' Ledger said without rancour. He
drank up his cocoa and went out to the upper deck and
headed for the torpedo tubes. Those tubes had been the late
TI's pride and joy and they all had names: Daisy, Ethel,
Agnes, Tina, Helen, Olga. In that order they spelled DEATHO
and each represented a chapter in the TI's love life. Leading
Seaman Ledger was phlegmatic when he learned that he was
suddenly to become a kind of torpedo instructor himself. A
gunner and a gunner's mate as his pupils, enough to make a
cat laugh, that was! They wouldn't be all that green, of
course, all they wanted was a run through to catch up on half-
forgotten knowledge. And if the tubes could bring this
mission off, well, it would be a fitting requiem for the TI, who
hadn't been a bad bloke to Ledger.

As he nattered away to his small class, Leading Seaman
Ledger could have fancied he was back in peacetime. It was
all quiet now and the sun had come out, thinly it was true, but
better than the snow. All the overcast had cleared away. They
would make a lovely target but the Jerries just weren't
bothering about them, which was strange. Cameron was
thinking the same thing. It was an unnatural calm; or was it?
Maybe the German command saw no point in risking more
aircraft: *Palatine* and *Probity* had given a pretty fair account

129

of themselves. The Nazis would know they had the ships in an iron grip. In time they would be starved out if nothing else. And when they moved, they could move only into the guns of Brest. Clearly, as he'd reflected earlier, the Germans were playing cat-and-mouse.

Cameron stiffened himself. Let them! It gave him time to make his own moves. He had reached a decision now and he sent down for the gunner.

'We'll give it a go, Guns. See to it that all six tubes are loaded and ready. I'll aim to pass in and out again, which will give both port and starboard mountings a chance. And in the meantime I'm landing an armed party. Sub-Lieutenant Hope will go away with thirty men . . . not in uniform, or not obviously in uniform,' he added, speaking to Harrison now. 'A touch of disguise on the surface. Understand?'

Harrison did: ratings landed without uniform would be in a poor way if captured, when they could be shot as spies. He said, 'The Resistance men who were killed aboard us. Use their clothing, sir.'

'Right. Hope'll take the *maquisards* with him – except for the two women. They want to get to England and nothing'll shift them from the ship.' Cameron looked at his watch. 'We'll be getting under way at full dark, and hope the landing parties will reach the outskirts of Brest not too long after we make the channel off Pointe de l'Armorique.'

'And after that?' Harrison asked.

Cameron said, 'We take it slow until we hear what I hope to hear – sounds of the *maquis* causing some noisy diversions around Brest. That's when we go in fast, pilotage consider-ations permitting, of course.' He took up his binoculars and swept the skies all around. It was all still very peaceful at first sight. But bringing the binoculars on to the shore where they had embarked Clémentine and her mother he saw a small movement behind some rising ground topped by tufty grass. Something black, something shiny, something that moved up and down – a uniform cap. He drew Harrison's attention to it. Harrison lifted an eyebrow and Cameron nodded.

130

'Oerlikons,' Harrison said. He passed an order and gave the target. The close-range weapons below the bridge on the starboard side opened in a sustained burst. Behind the tuft of grass bullets spattered around Hauptmann Schmelcher, arrived at last. He squirmed backwards until he was out of sight, muttering angrily and feeling immense fear. So like the British! But at least he knew where the Chalandon women had gone. They were trapped now. As he slid painfully to the rear Hauptmann Schmelcher's mind was busy. The first thing was the telephone at Laudevennec and a report to Brest; then a struggle back through the confounded snow-drifts – or the military could be ordered to provide a tracked vehicle from Laudevennec – and a salutary lesson to be taught to the people of Port Launay, where the guns would be out the moment he arrived back.

12

Cameron sent armed men away in the whaler to search for the man they had fired at. The whaler returned to the ship with a nil report: nothing to be seen. After that the landing parties were put ashore on the north bank of the Rivière de l'Hôpital, both *Probity*'s and *Palatine*'s whalers being used to ferry them across. The road around the water from the Rivière de l'Hôpital to Brest would be, according to Octavius, about thirty kilometres give or take a little. He would reckon to do it by not long after dark if he pushed the pace hard. Very hard, he admitted.

Sub-Lieutenant Hope had orders that were as precise as was possible in the circumstances but even so they left most of the initiative to him. That was inevitable, since no one could say what he would find in Brest. Broadly, with Leading Seaman Cusson as his second-in-command, he was to try to make contact with the marine commandos and cause a secondary diversion of his own – the main diversion would be up to Octavius and the men of the Resistance, who would split from the Naval party once they had the beginnings of Brest in sight. Octavius was confident that after making his own contact with the *maquisards* in the port he would be able to start a handy number of explosions and fires that would rattle the Boches badly.

As soon as the muster on shore was complete Hope started off along the road. Octavius had said there should be little traffic, all the petrol was earmarked for military transport and there was virtually no interchange between Brest and Landevennec. It would be different when they came close to the Naval installations further north and they would have to be ready to scatter; by that time the day would be darkening in any case. If they did happen to encounter any traffic before they were able to get off the track and into hiding, then they were to make a job of it with the automatic weapons and ensure that no one was left alive to make reports.

They were all dead tired – at least the Naval party were. No sleep since leaving Barry, except in odd snatches between bouts of action. Hope trudged on in the lead with Cusson bringing up the rear, their uniforms concealed beneath heavy jerseys, berets on their heads. No one had said it was a suicide mission, but Hope wasn't deluding himself for a moment. He wasn't going to see the UK again, not he nor any of the Naval party. The war was a bastard, a real bastard. The moment they neared Brest they would have had it. Well, no doubt they would be heroes back home but Hope knew, now, what it was like to be a condemned man, an inhabitant of Death Row. Just waiting for the chop – or rather, in this case, marching towards it. He recalled Number One's face when Cameron had been telling Cantley about the landing-party – Archer had been dead scared he was going to be named as officer in charge. The relief had been all too obvious. As for Hope, his heart had dropped into his boots but he hoped he hadn't shown it. Now he thought about Angela . . . the baby should be a consolation to her, he supposed.

Leading Seaman Cusson came up the line, his rifle at the short trail. 'Could you halt for a spell, sir?'

'What for?'

'One of the Frogs, sir. Got diarrhoea.'

'Can't he catch up?'

'Too old, sir. And lame with it.'

'Oh, all right,' Hope said. Cusson shouted the order and the column came to a halt. Cusson took out some Ticklers and a Rizla cigarette-rolling outfit. 'Permission to burn, sir?'

Hope nodded.

'You, sir?'

'Thanks.' Cusson rolled two cigarettes and they lit up. Hope said, 'I don't think we've got much hope. Do you?'

Cusson, lean-faced and dark-skinned, gave him a quick look. 'All the hope in the world, Mr Hope. Them Jerries, they'll be having the ships in mind but they won't be expecting us, attacking from the rear like. Element of surprise, sir. Works wonders! Like the bloke who's having a screw with someone else's missus and the someone else comes home unexpected like.' He gave a laugh, a reassuring one. Subby looked like a sick dog. It was all bollocks, what he'd been saying, but you didn't want defeatism to spread. You had to look confident, keep smiling, like the poor sods in the Flanders mud in the last war. But he saw the officer didn't believe him for a moment. Hope was as good as dead already, in his mind. When the Resistance man had finished and rejoined from behind a bush, they moved on again, fast. Cusson wondered about the Frog: clean ship's water to blame most likely – not used to it, stomach adjusted to plenty of germs and that. It was a weird world sometimes; Cusson remembered one of his cousins saying not long before that none of the people in their home village near Macclesfield, when serving abroad in crappy places, Egypt or the western desert for instance, had ever suffered from wog tummy, commonly known as the runs. Suez Canal even, where almost everyone who just passed through without even landing for a second got the runs badly. The reason? His cousin, who worked in the sanitary inspector's office in Macclesfield, had told him. The cottages clustered round the gates of the local big house had all used the village well for their water supply. Just before the war started it had been discovered that the drains from the big house had been leaking for bloody years past into the well. All that muck had given them an immunity. Funny, that! Too much hygiene was a bad thing. Cusson had often felt like telling officers that story, when they made their rounds and poked into everything to ensure cleanliness, the heads especially.

Some miles behind the column a curious vehicle, a staff car

134

fitted with caterpillar tracks, was coming up from Port Launay via Landevennec. This vehicle contained Hauptmann Schmelcher, who knew nothing of the French and British ahead of him. Schmelcher sat in the back, cap on his head, staring bleakly over his driver's shoulder. And feeling a worm of anxiety in his guts. There was, he knew, trouble of a sensational nature ahead. In Port Launay he had been about to make a number of arrests, exemplary ones, of the inhabitants and to ask a number of questions which he knew they wouldn't answer, thus giving him the excuse for bad treatment. But before he could do so his telephone had rung and he had been ordered to present himself to the Gestapo HQ in Brest. At once; and the voice on the phone had held an obvious threat. The Gestapo were not immune to threatening their own when one of them stepped out of line or showed a lack of zeal or intelligence – nor were they immune to feelings of jealousy and it was not unknown for the higher officers to indulge in vendettas against those of lesser rank who had shown excessive zeal and thus might undermine their own positions by being promoted; Schmelcher was in his own view one of these, but it was curious and alarming that the summons should come close on the heels of the escape of the *maquisards* from Port Launay.

The military transport went on as fast as the state of the road would permit. Schmelcher must not be late. Brooding now, he didn't hear his driver the first time.

'What did you say, Götz?'

'Men, Herr Hauptmann! On the road ahead, in the distance – '

'What men?' Schmelcher craned forward.

'I think they are the accursed *maquisards*, Herr Hauptmann.'

Schmelcher swore and brought out his revolver. He had seen them for himself now. So many of them, in black berets and jerseys. The undoubted look of the wretched Resistance! But he couldn't turn back. To do so would be held against him in Brest. This was a time for courage. 'Drive through them,' he snapped. 'Use your revolver, Götz.'

'*Jawohl*, Herr Hauptmann.'

The tracked vehicle lumbered on. A moment later it had been heard. Leading Seaman Cusson yelled at the men to clear the track and be ready with their automatic weapons. The Frenchmen and Naval ratings moved fast, jumping aside. When he was within range Schmelcher fired through his window, aiming at armed men seen intermittently behind the trees; Götz in front smashed away the windscreen and fired too, but the French weapons had the advantage. Götz fell sideways behind the wheel and the vehicle slewed hard to the right and smashed into a tree. One of the tracks came off with a look of finality. A hole appeared in the canvas roof and through it flew Hauptmann Schmelcher, minus his cap and revolver, to land in a heap close to Octavius. Octavius gave him a kick, and he squealed. 'He is alive,' the Frenchman said to Sub-Lieutenant Hope. 'Also not very injured, which is surprising.' He bent and jerked Schmelcher to his feet. The Gestapo man stared into a ring of guns. He licked his lips but said nothing. Octavius did the talking, using a curious mixture of French, English and German. Hope got the drift of it: the Gestapo man was in for a bad time if he didn't answer a few questions. He was going to be given a taste of his own medicine.

He was. Nobody took any notice when Hope and Cusson protested, except to tell them that this was Frenchmen's business. The French had suffered under Hitler's Gestapo, the British hadn't, not yet. Hope saw the point and turned his back on what was going to happen. Better if the British Navy wasn't involved . . . the men of the Resistance, the *maquisards* so hated and feared by the Gestapo, removed Hauptmann Schmelcher's breeches, let them dangle over the tops of his knee-boots, lifted his shirt and jacket and produced a knife. The threat was obvious and Schmelcher knew it would be carried out. The hatred was so mutual and some terrible things had been done, things that Hauptmann Schmelcher now very much wished had not been. And there

136

was certainty in his mind on one point: never would he sacrifice his manhood for his Führer. It was asking too much. He talked. The trek for Brest was resumed with very little delay, Hauptmann Schmelcher accompanying the *maquisards* very closely guarded, and the wrecked staff car with its dead driver being left in the trees.

Octavius had words with Hope. '*M'sieur*, there has been some help given. It is a fact, it seems, that the airfields near Brest have been heavily attacked this morning. There has been severe damage.'

Hope asked, 'Can he be believed?'

'I think so,' Octavius answered quietly and with confidence. 'Because he is still with us and will remain so. That was not all he had to say. He has passed word to Brest by telephone, to say the British ships are off Landevennec and one is sunk. He does not believe any German warships will be sent in from the port of Brest, but rather that your ship will be sealed in.'

Hope nodded; this was what the Captain had believed too. But Hauptmann Schmelcher had revealed something else when asked, and this was that he had received a report that many of the marine commandos were alive still, their whereabouts unknown. All authorities in the Rade area had been warned to be on the watch for them, though it was believed they were still in the close vicinity of Brest and probably receiving help and shelter from the Resistance. There was a very active military and Gestapo presence in every area of the town.

'But we shall still get through,' Octavius said. 'It is no exaggeration to say that the *maquisards* outnumber the German garrison.'

'And they have the arms?'

'*Oui m'sieur*, they have the arms.'

But they're not an army, Hope thought, with misgivings in plenty. They're not formed up for attack. They didn't operate that way, presumably. Strictly underground – except, of course, for that storming of the quay before the British ships

137

had pulled out from Brest. But when asked Octavius didn't think that would be repeated. There were, he said, many other ways: and he refused to be drawn further than that. Hope got the idea the men of the Resistance didn't care to confide too much in the British, who might be taken by the Germans and might not possess quite the steely determination of the *maquis* never to talk of what they knew.

Fair enough point, Hope thought. His own resolve had never been tested in the way that of the French had. He didn't believe he would be able to withstand torture himself. But, of course, the Germans were bound by the Geneva Convention as to treatment and interrogation of prisoners-of-war and there was no evidence that they had ever broken faith with that. Hope put the point to Octavius, who simply spat on the ground. The Boches were pigs, capable of anything when it suited their book.

The move on Brest continued as the wintry sun climbed towards noon. The men were impeded by the lying snow that had yielded only a little to the raised temperature of morning and it soon became obvious that they were going to be late on their ETA outside Brest. As the day wore on the sun would go and the snow would harden again and become slippery, although they might well make better speed when their legs no longer sank at every step. There was in fact more snow lying as they went north, more than they had found further back. It was for this reason that Schmelcher knew he could place no reliance on a party being sent from Brest to find out why he had not reported as ordered – they would know in Brest what the road conditions would be like. They wouldn't be able to get through themselves either. His lips a thin line of bloodlessness Schmelcher struggled on, surrounded by guns, cruelly aware that he would be written off for many hours to come as lost in a snow-drift . . .

Back to the south-west aboard *Probity*, all remaining hands were still closed up at action stations, permission being given for men to take turns to snatch some sleep at the guns and torpedo-tubes, the latter now ready for their forthcoming night's work under the aegis of Mr Cantley and the gunner's mate. Time was much on Cameron's mind: he could visualize the difficulties of a forced march of twenty miles – it would be bad enough without the snow. There might be a longer wait than he'd bargained for off the entry to the Rade.

He said this to Harrison.

'Can't be helped, sir,' Harrison said.

'No. But every moment increases the danger. They're going to pick up the ship's northward movement on their radar – we can't assume the station the Resistance put out of action was the only one the Germans had, although I suppose it might have been. We're going to need something else.'

'But what?'

Cameron said, 'That signal in the night. I'm certain there's a British presence somewhere outside, probably a good way off, but reasonably handy – right?'

'Yes, sir. All right so far. But – '

'They can be contacted, Harrison.'

Harrison was doubtful. 'By using our w/t, sir?'

'Yes, why not? There's no bloody secrecy to be lost now, is there?'

'Doesn't that rather depend when you use it, sir?'

Cameron said, 'Frankly, no. I can't see that it does. Not from a secrecy angle, that is – and I repeat, that's all gone for a burton in any case. I take the timing point, though, from a different aspect: we have to make wireless contact at the right moment for the operation itself. That's important.'

Harrison was looking puzzled. 'I don't quite follow, sir.'

Cameron grinned. 'Easy! I want to alert our unknown friend out there as to what I intend to do – torpedo the U-boat shelters. And I want him to create a diversion of his own, add to the general confusion, take the Jerry minds off both us and the Resistance – at the right moment. Follow now?'

Harrison did. He said, 'And if the Resistance and our chaps don't get there in time – '

'Exactly, yes. I doubt if we can bring it off without either the one or the other. Both would be better. That's when the

139

time query comes in. Exactly when do we make the signal?'

'And,' Harrison said, 'what, exactly, do we say? Without being too exact!'

Cameron said, 'We'll have a word with your PO Tel and mine. A little combined brainwork. What I'm aiming for is to have that ship pretty close to the entrance to the Goulet by 2000 hours at the latest. I think we can reckon on the shore party making Brest by then, if ever they make it at all. By that time I shall be close south of Ile Longue. The rest of it's guesswork – because we don't know that ship's position, how long it's going to take her to close the Goulet.'

The two petty officers were sent for: Gander ex-*Palatine* and PO Telegraphist Lock of *Probity*. Lock was a cadaverous man with a completely bald head, two good-conduct badges beneath his PO's crossed fouled anchors, three children and like Leading Seaman McNee a strong religious sense. He had been tickled pink at the use of the Bible to announce support in the vicinity. He knew, as a long-serving rating, that admirals and captains and such did make frequent use of the Bible in signal traffic, mainly for visual signalling but the principle was the same, and they made use of it in a jokey sort of way. That he didn't approve of, but on this occasion God had not been mocked. He added his head to those of Cameron and Gander and *Probity*'s acting skipper and cudgelled his brain for a Biblical reference that would cover all aspects of the night operational requirements. Not surprisingly, he didn't succeed. After a good deal of hard thought he reckoned you'd need an archbishop. No one else had any ideas either. Then something clicked in Lock's mind and he asked, 'What actual time was it you wanted the ship concerned to be off the Goulet, sir? 2000 hours, was it?'

'That's right.'

Lock said, sounding triumphant, '*Monday Night at Eight*, sir!'

'Yes. It being Monday – yes.'

Lock said, 'You've not ticked over, sir. Ridiculous Urry.'

'Oh, for God's sake, Lock! What about a ridiculous hurry?'

140

'Nor hurry, sir. *Urry. Monday Night at Eight*, sir – BBC. Nicholas Ridiculous, played by Jacques Brown. And Leonard Urry with the BBC Variety Orchestra – got it? Regular as clockwork, sir, every Monday night – '

'Yes, all right, Lock. I know all that. *Ridiculous Urry . . .* you're suggesting making that as the signal?'

'That's right, sir.'

'Well, it has the right sort of ring to it! But it doesn't really convey much, does it?'

'Not to the Jerries . . . and that's the idea. I agree it really needs a bit more attached like, but that's just what we can't risk doing. That's if we made it to this ship that sent the signal. But make it to the *Admiralty*, sir – they'd tick over in a flash that we're going to do something at 2000 hours and we're asking for assistance. Read our minds and pass the right orders to the ship on station, using Naval cypher, all nice and secure, sir.'

Cameron looked at Harrison. They both laughed. Cameron said, 'Well done, PO. It's full of holes . . . yet at the same time it's watertight in a weird sort of way.'

Lock looked gratified. 'When will you want the signal made, sir?'

'Right away, PO. Give the Admiralty time for thought! If they tick over as hoped, they'll be the ones to know exactly when to order the assistance in on a closing course for the Goulet.'

Harrison said, 'You can help with a prayer, Lock.'

'Aye, aye, sir. Come to just the right man, sir.'

As the petty officers left the bridge Cameron found he wasn't as sanguine as he had perhaps appeared. The wizards at the Admiralty were going to have to read one hell of a lot into two words. But they were bound to react to the significance of any transmission from the ships of Operation Scatter in their current situation – their known situation, thanks to the Resistance radio operators.

Back in the transmitting room, Petty Officer Telegraphist Lock checked the Safe to Transmit board, settled himself into his chair for what was to be the most vital signal of his career, and sent out the call sign of the Admiralty in London. When the acknowledgement came back he made his brief transmission with the identification of *Probity* included in it. The signal was, as expected, picked up by eavesdroppers in the Naval dockyard at Brest and reported. It caused much excitement and more than a dozen different interpretations were placed upon it, none of them accurate. German Naval officers, coding and cyphering experts, were brought in to consider the meaning. Chins were pulled, eyes were narrowed, tempers lost.

No use: it meant nothing. It could be a corrupt group. The wireless installations listened for a repeat, but nothing more was heard. The whole thing could have been a mistake; the Germans railed away at the French officers, stupid fellows as bad as the British, who were renowned *dumkopfs*. The thought of looking at a copy of the *Radio Times*, which by order of Herr Docktor Goebbels was always obtained from his agents in the BBC and distributed to the various German commands, occurred to no one. But in the Admiralty the so-stupid British did a little better. When duty permitted they were all avid listeners to the BBC's regular programmes. *ITMA* with Tommy Handley . . . there were so many Colonel Chinstraps around and Mrs Mopp's real-life proto-type could be seen any day, in any government department, moving on bunioned feet with mop and bucket: 'Can I do yer now, sir?' *Monday Night at Eight* was equally popular and at once the two names rang a bell. Something, therefore, was scheduled for 2000 hours and it had to be assumed in the absence of any further information that it did in fact mean this very night – Monday. What was left of Operation Scatter was asking for the assistance of the warship that had been ordered south from the Clyde and had made W/T contact during the night.

It couldn't have been clearer. The plea for help was so obvious; *Probity* wouldn't have risked a transmission if she hadn't been asking for assistance. There would have been absolutely no point.

The duty captain authorized the signal without reference to higher authority. He ordered, 'w/t cypher to *Glamorgan* . . . she's to close the French coast so as to be off the Goulet de Brest at 2000 hours tonight . . . thereafter she's to react to events as required by Senior Officer Operation Scatter.'

13

As the early dusk of winter settled over the Rade de Brest the weary Naval party in its disguise, and the genuine *maquisards*, were marching still. There had been no more snow; but the night promised to be very cold and it might snow again – either that or rain. The overcast had come back as the sun went down. The men trudged on, taking Hauptmann Schmelcher with them. He was almost dead on his feet; he was not used to this sort of thing, he always travelled by comfortable car or sometimes less comfortable truck – he walked only short distances, partly because he was forever fearful of a knife in the back. Now the fear was very present; it was likely he had only a short time to live. These wicked people would be without mercy. But he didn't want to make the time any shorter so he had decided to give his full co-operation and then, when he saw his moment, he would escape. The *maquisards* would soon have other matters on their minds and their vigilance would relax; he was sure of that. Then afterwards he would have to make up some satisfactory story as to how it was he had allowed himself, an officer of the famed and revered Gestapo, to be captured by riff-raff. But that could wait. Lies came easily enough to Hauptmann Schmelcher and there would be little difficulty.

In the meantime he would cringe. In the meantime he would do as he had been asked – told – and do what he could to help the riff-raff enter Brest unmolested, or at least give them a full briefing as to what his experience told him would be the Fatherland's military dispositions since the dastardly

144

attack on the U-boat shelters, so that they could avoid them. Not that he believed they could have any success whatsoever, for which fact, if he couldn't get away in time, they would blame him. Nevertheless, he was to be a hostage of a sort and he could well recognize the advantages to himself inherent in that role. They wouldn't want to kill him so long as he had a use.

A couple of hours after dark they were not so far off the distant outskirts of the port and so far there had been no encounters with German troops. Sub-Lieutenant Hope's heart was thumping like a steam hammer as they closed towards unknown dangers. He hoped desperately that *Probity* would now be under way, that nothing had occurred to stop her steaming up towards Ile Longue and Pointe de l'Armorique with her guns and torpedo-tubes manned and ready. He was very conscious that a lot of it was going to be up to him, that the eastward diversion was part and parcel of the Captain's plan, but he knew too that any diversion he could cause – unless they found the commandos and their explosive charges – was going to be dependent upon sheer luck. The Resistance men knew where to go, of course, for the best advantage, but the difficulty lay not in selection but in reaching the target before being slaughtered by the German machine-guns and rifles . . .

As he worried, as fear nagged at him, Octavius drew alongside him. 'You are nervous, *mon ami*.'

'No . . .'

There was a laugh. 'Confess it and you will feel better! Me, I am nervous too. We are all afraid. We put it behind us when the time comes to fight. So will you! And do not doubt that we shall succeed. We know our country, we know Brest – and we have learned to know the Boches.' Octavius paused. 'You have not seen this kind of fighting before, *m'sieur*?'

'No,' Hope said.

'Nor any others from your ships. You are seamen. I think you will learn quite a lot tonight, *m'sieur*. The work of the Resistance has to be done in many ways, ways that would not be used, perhaps, by armies fighting openly on the field of battle. We have been forced into this by the actions of the Boches, and of the Gestapo very particularly. But you will see, *m'sieur*. Now I shall tell you what our first objective is – that is, the objective of the men of the *maquis*, when they part from your men, which will be soon now.' Octavius laid a hand on Hope's shoulder. 'Do not be worried. Two of our number will remain with your seamen as guides. I shall be one.'

'I'm glad to hear it! And the objective – the objective of the *maquis*?'

Octavius said, 'On the eastern outskirts of Brest there is a bridge that crosses the northern arm of the Rade. This shortens the journey – but that is by the way. On the northern side of the bridge there is a temporary ammunition dump, temporary in the sense that the Boches use it as a half-way house for supplies brought down from Germany. It is no more than a big shed, *m'sieur*, and the stock lies about openly, awaiting removal to the main arsenal in the dockyard. Two days ago an ammunition train reached Brest, and this temporary dump is full. That is our first objective, to blow it up.'

Hope said, 'Surely it'll be well guarded, *m'sieur*?'

'Oh, yes! Very well guarded certainly. But not against Hauptmann Schmelcher – '

'The Gestapo man? But how – '

'You will see. We have been fortunate – had not the pig Schmelcher fallen into our hands . . . then I would not have thought it possible to approach the dump. For now I shall say no more, except that your seamen will cross the bridge with all of us, and we part company on the other side.'

Octavius made his way ahead, rejoining his own contingent which had by this time moved into the lead. The night was quiet; and the expected rain was starting now. Hope felt the cold drops on his skin, heralding the downpour. Soon it came in buckets, penetrating all clothing. It seemed to darken the already dark night; Brest, blacked out as it was, lay invisibly threatening, now not far ahead. From time to time during the last part of the march they had had to clear the road as dimmed headlights were seen, and lie silent in ditches or behind the trees. But now there was no movement at all other than their own, no sound except for the hiss of the rain, the footfalls of the men and heavy breathing.

Soon the word came back from Octavius in the lead: the bridge was close. In two minutes the Naval party was to halt, and the *maquisards* would go forward, fast-moving shadows in the night, and when Octavius made a sound as of a dog barking, Hope's seamen would move on again at the double.

Behind the landward party, still away to the south of Ile Longue, *Probity* was now under way and moving up the dark, rain-splashed waters of the Rade de Brest. It was full high water and this time the pilotage was easier; no boat had been sent away to take soundings. Cameron stood silent against the fore rails, staring into the blackness through binoculars, ready to take over the handling of the ship from Harrison once they were coming through between Ile Longue and Pointe de l'Armorique. His thoughts were bleak: he had disliked leaving the pathetic, stricken jags of *Palatine* behind. So short a time in command – but no one liked to lose his ship. There was one consolation in what had been an unavoidable act: the poor old *Palatine* had no equipment of any interest to the Germans so there was no question of breaching security by what had had to be left, no need to carry out further acts of destruction to finish off the bombers' work.

On the iron-deck below the funnels Mr Cantley stood ready with the port side mounting and its three torpedo tubes with the lethal fish in place. Petty Officer Todd stood by to starboard, already waiting the firing order from the fore-bridge. He knew he would have some while to wait yet and he was finding the wait bad for the nerves. This thought he found funny in itself: no one on the lower deck would ever believe a gunner's mate had a nerve in his body. Gunner's mates were popularly supposed to be made of non-combustible material, no feelings, and had been quarried rather than born of woman. It was an image that many of the fraternity cultivated assiduously, hence its widespread acceptance.

From Number Three gun Stripey Trudge, co-opted to take the place of one of *Probity*'s dead gunnery rates, looked down on the torpedo-tubes to either side, just visible through the gloom. Deadly buggers . . . it had been fish that had got the old *Royal Oak*, inside the boom at Scapa. If those fish did happen to enter the U-boat shelters there was going to be an inferno, but Stripey didn't believe they would have that much luck, not them. The fish would take the outer wall and as like as not go up close and fling chunks of stone down on *Probity* and on him. He gave a shiver of apprehension. If the skipper was just an inch out when he gave the firing order, or if that Cantley or the GI was slow to react, they would all be pierced by millions of little stone slivers. To say nothing of what the Jerries were going to sling at them the moment they were spotted.

A nasty situation to be in, on an able seaman's rate of pay plus miserable allowances, which didn't come to a lot to fight for King and country on. And die. But you had to be philosophical about it. There wasn't a lot to old age either. Stripey Trudge remembered both his grand-dads, curmudgeons the two of them, as bad as each other, moan and drip all day long, saying the young 'uns were no good, taking out their false teeth for comfort and chewing on bare gums as though they couldn't stop, eyes glittering ready to find the next fault. One of them, his mum's dad, had remembered Balaclava and the charge of the Light Brigade – hadn't been there, but remembered it being talked about, and ended his days still talking about it just as though he *had* been there.

Stripey didn't want to end up like that, chuntering on and on to dwindling audiences about what he'd done at Brest one night long ago, boring mutinous grandchildren whose only wish would be that grand-dad should turn his toes up and call it a day . . . suddenly Stripey's stomach loosened. It was too soon to go yet. He wasn't old by a long chalk. Life began to

148

beckon again, strongly.

The bridge personnel were all as taut as violin strings. Cameron looked again and again at his watch, set to the ship's chronometers, wondered where the support ship was, whether or not the Admiralty had ticked over. A number of Admiralty signals had been picked up since *Probity*'s own transmission, but without the decyphering tables and the basic Naval cypher they hadn't been transcribable, while the call signs conveyed nothing in particular – the Admiralty was always pushing out signal traffic, operational orders and routines. They'd made no reply to *Probity* and Cameron had expected none. If the Nazis knew their call sign, they would at once smell a rat and link the reply in with the original two-word signal.

The time again: 1950 hours.

Harrison said, 'Ile Longue's coming up now. Fine on the port bow.'

Looking through his binoculars again, Cameron said, 'Don't forget *Panoply*, Harrison.'

'She's well in mind, sir.'

Cameron nodded. Ile Longue loomed through the darkness. Across the channel, Pointe de l'Armorique could not yet be seen. But not long to go now . . . blood drummed through Cameron's head. The pilotage was tricky, very tricky with the sunken wrecks of French and German ships now added to by *Panoply*'s shattered hulk lying half across the channel. Harrison was forced to reduce speed as Ile Longue came closer. They could quickly cram it on again and for the moment considerations of pilotage had to come first. In the wheelhouse *Probity*'s coxswain repeated the helm and engine orders up the voice-pipe, watched by Chief Petty Officer King who was with him as a back-up number, a replacement if and when necessary. Tiny King was thinking of his kids, with his parents in Rowlands Castle outside Pompey, behind Portsdown Hill. While he'd been buggering about all day in the Rade de Brest the Nazis might have been over Pompey, dropping their incendiaries and high explosive. His family

149

could have been in Pompey, taking it all. Land mines, too. It had been a land mine that had got the chief and petty officers' mess in the barracks one night, and the morning had revealed sheer horror, any number of old shipmates from pre-war commissions lying gutted and without arms or legs, spewed up with the wreckage. Didn't bear thinking about, but King, with nothing to do currently but watch and wait, couldn't shut out home and the things that could happen at any moment during a war . . . but something else was going to happen any moment too, happen to himself, and then how about the kids and his old mum and dad? The old lady, he knew, would never accept it. She would go on waiting for him to get off the train from Pompey and come round the corner by Wigginton and Hern the grocers, past the post office and the Railway Hotel and the Fountain Inn and across the village green towards Redhill Road . . . .

Probity's coxswain glanced across at him. 'Thinking of the sprogs,' he said. Ted Andrews had known Tiny King's wife, knew all the family; he and King had served a commission together in the Home Fleet destroyers before the war, and when both their ships had come into Portsmouth from time to time, King had asked him round, happy times they'd been . . . and it was one of the better things about being called back from reserve that you met so many old friends again.

'That obvious, is it?' King asked.

Andrews didn't answer. The skipper was manoeuvring now, the helm being ordered this way and that as *Probity* felt her way round the obstructions. This was a bad moment: not far off the port – the searchlights might come on and show the ship up like day and then everything would open long before she could make the turn to starboard for the run past the U-boat pens, the last turn Andrews believed she would ever make.

Ashore by the Rade's northern arm, the stretch of water that ran east-nor'-easterly from the port itself, the advance on the bridge had been swift, silent and deadly. There were guards at either end; the guard on the northern end heard nothing of what had happened to his opposite number. Two *maquisards* had seized the man, a hand had clamped around his mouth and a knife had been slid into his back; he died soundlessly and at once. Then a number of shadows had gone across and the second Nazi had died in a similar fashion, and Octavius had made his barking-dog signal. When all the party was across together with Hauptmann Schmelcher, there came the parting of the ways. The two Resistance men, Octavius as promised being one, led Sub-Lieutenant Hope and his party westwards while the remainder of the *maquis* made their silent advance on the ammunition dump. Hope asked Octavius where he was heading.

'A friend,' Octavius said. He would say nothing more explicit than that. He moved fast, sliding into the outskirts. There was no apparent German activity yet. That could be due to a number of possibilities, Hope thought. The support ship could have been picked up – she might have moved in closer by now – or *Probity*'s movement might have been seen and the Nazis were standing by in the port area. On the other hand the landing party could be moving into a trap; but whatever it was the Resistance men seemed unworried and it was not long before the party was moving through a maze of small streets, narrow streets with an appalling amount of bomb damage. There was a smell of death in the air. Dogs and cats roamed hungrily, ragged men and women were seen now and then in the wreckage, looking as though they had emerged from some hole in the ground. They took no notice of the group of men passing by. After ten minutes Octavius halted near a half-ruined building, little more than a shell, a building that seemed to have been a cinema or theatre. Along one remaining wall what looked like banks of seats rose dimly, just visible as an outline, but there was little else. The stage or screen had vanished in piles of rubble.

Octavius led the way into the wreckage. Once again he emulated a barking dog. He waited, then repeated the sound. Away to his left some rubble fell, making everyone swing

151

round with their rifles ready. There was a short pause then footsteps were heard and more debris fell. A voice from the darkness said something in French and was responded to by Octavius – an exchange of passwords, Hope supposed. There was a low conversation then Octavius said to Hope, 'Come, follow me, *m'sieur.*'

They picked their way through the ruination behind the Resistance man. They were led to a corner of the building and through a gap into a courtyard behind, a square place also full of rubble and with a renewed stench of death, perhaps from corpses still buried somewhere beneath the fallen masonry. Scrambling and slipping about as the rain sliced down, they crossed to the far side of the courtyard to where there was a manhole cover set in the ground and half covered with debris. The man who had answered Octavius' barking sound, a thick-set man with shoulders like a wrestler's, rippling muscles and the inevitable beret, bent and lifted the iron cover. Octavius went down, feet groping apparently for ladder rungs, and one by one they all followed, leaving the thick-set man behind. Leading Seaman Cusson said as he reached the bottom of the ladder, 'Well, stone me, it's a flaming sewer! Talk about stink.' They moved on away from the ladder, with a torch now lighting the sewer ahead. They moved along a raised bank, with filthy water moving sluggishly beneath in the channel of the sewer. Hope felt he was going to be sick at any moment, and held a handkerchief over his nose. The stench seemed even to invade his throat when he breathed through his mouth, thick, heavy and horrible. After what seemed an age, they reached a section that widened out quite considerably, at the bottom of another steel ladder reaching into the overhead gloom, its end lost to sight from below. In this section four men stood, each carrying a sub-machine-gun. They had a taut, watchful look as though those guns might be used at any moment, and they said nothing. Here in this space, the party was halted. Hope asked where they were in relation to the world above.

Octavius said, 'Here we are beneath the main part of Brest.

We are close to the port area.'

'What do we do now?'

'We wait, *m'sieur*. We wait . . . arrangements are being made with others of the Resistance. That is one thing we wait for. There is another.'

'What's that?'

In the glow from the torch Hope saw the smile on the man's face. Octavius said, 'We wait for Hauptmann Schmelcher. That is the other thing we wait for.'

'Schmelcher? But – '

'You will see. Have patience, *m'sieur*. It should not be long now.'

14

Hauptmann Schmelcher did not keep anyone waiting for very much longer. Schmelcher, though by now his hands had been tied tightly behind his back by the wretched *maquisards*, was running very fast for the safety of the ammunition dump. His mind was in a ferment: the Frenchmen had let him go, amazingly.

There was something Schmelcher was not fully aware of. As he ran like the wind for safety it was true that he felt something bumping up and down on his rump, beneath his tied hands, but that was all he knew and this was not the time for asking questions, so he just ran.

Secured to his leather belt was a heavy package.

In the package were two hand grenades and two Molotov cocktails, petrol bombs in wine bottles that would spurt out flame when ignited. The pins of the hand grenades had been withdrawn just as Schmelcher had started off. The hauptmann shouted as he ran, shouted himself hoarse, and a torch beamed out and lit on the black uniform of the Gestapo and quickly the gate was flung open and so was the door of the big shed-like structure housing the ammunition store. As Schmelcher slowed inside the gate, bullets zipped across from the *maquisards* and Schmelcher ran on fast again, cursing. The door of the ammunition store was opened briefly to admit him to safety. He plunged through like a maniac. And as the door was shut behind him Hauptmann Schmelcher exploded. Seconds later so did the ammunition. The place became an inferno. There was nothing left of Hauptmann Schmelcher;

even his badges had melted.

The result of Schmelcher's activities was heard in the sewer – heard and felt as shock waves travelled through the earth. There was a noticeable tremor accompanied by a hollow booming sound, and the ladder running up to the manhole cover shook slightly. Octavius said, 'That was Schmelcher.'

'How, Schmelcher?' Hope asked, bewildered.

'He was acting as a human bomb, *m'sieur*.' Octavius explained in detail. Hope felt a sense of horror but recalled the Resistance man's earlier words, that the British had not suffered like the French. Octavius went on, 'That was the first diversion. Perhaps the only one we shall be able to achieve, but it will have had its effect on the Boches. Now there is the next thing: your marine commandos.'

'Do you know what has happened to them?'

Octavius said, 'Yes, *m'sieur*, I know now. My comrade of the *maquis*, the one who met us at the sewer entry – he told me. We must reach them fast. Thirty men are left and have been hidden by the Resistance, and the Resistance had of course no knowledge of what you, the British, intended to do.'

'You mean re-enter the port – '

'I mean, *m'sieur*, the use of torpedoes against the U-boat shelters. Your commandos are in another sector of the sewage system, one that has been sealed off for some time now from the main flow because of the building of the bomb-proof shelters and the U-boat pens, which run deep.' Octavius paused, staring at the sub-lieutenant in the light from the torch. '*M'sieur*, they are safe only until your captain fires the torpedoes. Their hiding place is close up beside the shelters, beside the target of your captain.'

Octavius went on to say that to reach the sealed-off sector they would need to emerge from the main sewer and move through the streets; and that they must wait for the arrival of a certain person first. He added, 'The Boches know where the commandos are hiding, and there is a guard on the sewer entry. The Boches will wait for a surrender when starvation presses. They know, you see, that the commandos have their weapons intact – '

'And their explosive charges?'

Octavius nodded. '*Oui, m'sieur*. And the Boches, they will not take unnecessary risks. They are confident the commandos cannot hope to get away – but we believe that we can get them out. The man we now await – he is an operative of the sewage system and we hope he will be able to find another way of reaching your soldiers, a way not known to the Boches.'

Sweating, Hope looked at his watch: 2015. *Probity* would be moving through into the Goulet at any moment. He said, 'We should try to warn the ship. I don't see how, but – '

'*Non, m'sieur*! There must not be interference now . . . and I think your captain would not hold his action back. In war targets must be hit, and men must die.'

The explosion had lit the sky with red and orange, great tongues of flame that leapt above the rolling clouds of thick black smoke. For a moment the whole port of Brest was outlined starkly; as the main explosion died and was followed by a number of smaller ones the glow remained in the northeast to prove a help to ship-handling. There would be considerable alarm now on the part of the Germans. All the same, the diversion had come a shade too soon. *Probity* had been outlined, shown up along with the port installations even if only momentarily, and now the searchlights were busy. Two of them picked the ship up, and steadied, holding her in the beams. The Germans were not so disorganized as Cameron had hoped. There were warships lying off the U-boat pens, as if in protection, and in the instant that the order was passed to the guns to open with the searchlights as their targets, the enemy fire started. The German gunnery was good: there was a massive explosion right overhead and the forebridge was filled with flying splinters. Cameron staggered back against the chart table at the after end of the forebridge, blood streaming from his left shoulder and an agonizing pain

156

shooting down the arm and across his chest. In the director Midshipman Richards with *Probity*'s director layer had been torn apart; the director itself was gone, blasted from its tripod to smash on to the fore funnel from which it hung for a moment before crashing down to the deck amidships.

Cameron came upright, glanced down at the deck. Harrison lay in a heap beside the binnacle, very still, with his mouth hanging open. The yeoman of signals was nowhere to be seen. Someone was calling urgently up the voice-pipe from the wheelhouse: the coxswain.

'Forebridge! Are you all right up there, sir?'

'I'm all right, cox'n. Is Chief Petty Officer King still there?'

'Yes, sir – '

'Send him up. I've got the ship.' Cameron took a deep breath. 'I'm taking her out to sea for now and hope to contact our support ship. The Nazis have a concentration of frigates off the shelters.'

'Aye, aye, sir.'

King came up to the bridge. Cameron conned the ship up Ile Longue, passing close by the remains of *Panoply*. It was a squeeze to get through and as they came north they were more and more at the mercy of the Nazi shore batteries and the guns of the frigates lying off the pens. The whole plan seemed to have fallen apart now. The din was tremendous, battering away at the eardrums, light was everywhere, light and sound and fury, the whole of the port area seeming to be ablaze as the destroyer fought towards the Goulet for the outward passage. Her guns were firing back, so fast that if it was kept up the barrels would run red hot. Two of the searchlights went out as Cameron, reaching the extremity of Pointe des Espagnols, increased speed.

'Full ahead both engines, port fifteen.'

'Full ahead both engines, sir. Fifteen of port wheel on, sir.'

Disregarding the bombardment, Cameron watched his bearings closely. 'Midships.'

'Midships, sir. Wheel's amidships, sir. Course, two-four-five, sir.'

'Steer two-four-oh.'

'Steer two-four-oh, sir.'

Cameron was glad of the steady, phlegmatic responses. Just as though no one was firing at them. He was glad of the presence of Chief PO King on the bridge. King said, 'I don't think it was ever a winner, sir.'

'The torpedoing?'

'That too, sir. What I meant was, the whole ruddy show. Admiralty being too clever by half, sir.'

Cameron nodded; he tended to agree but he wasn't going to accept defeat yet. He was going to come back in. He said, 'Check for damage, please, Cox'n.'

'Aye, aye, sir.' King went fast down the ladder. He found the First Lieutenant coming for'ard along the iron deck at the double. He asked, 'What's it like, sir?'

'The ack-ack's gone. Direct hit. How's the bridge? I was on my way – '

'Bridge is all right, sir, Lieutenant-Commander Cameron in full charge. Lieutenant Harrison and the yeoman dead. We're moving out, just for now, sir.'

Archer nodded and was moving on for the bridge ladder when the sound of gunfire and a flash of light came from ahead and something heavy exploded on the north shore of the Goulet behind the racing destroyer. From aft they heard the gunner's shout: 'Six-inch, I reckon! They've sent a bloody cruiser, thanks be to God!'

On shore to the east Hope was waiting still, a prey to gnawing anxiety, wondering what *Probity* was doing. She couldn't have fired off her torpedoes – the result would probably have broken the whole sewer network wide open – and that meant she was late on her ETA. Anything might have happened out there in the fresh air, she could have been sunk. Noise was coming down to them but it was hard to identify. It could be continuing explosions from the ammunition dump or it could be gunfire. Hope believed it was the latter. If so, then *Probity* would be in the thick of it and the whole thing had miscarried

– which left him down a sewer, him and all the others.

Leading Seaman Cusson was philosophic about it. 'Safe here, sir. Bad air has its compensations, eh?'

'Safe until the Nazis find us.'

'POW camp, sir. There's worse things.'

'Are you married, Cusson?'

'No, sir. I see what you mean . . . married yourself, do I take it, sir?'

Hope said yes, he was. He didn't say any more on the subject; somehow he didn't want to discuss approaching fatherhood and its attendant anxieties, a sewer didn't seem the place for that, sitting there like rats beneath what was going on overhead, but he was worrying badly about Angela. It wouldn't be long before the BBC came up with a bulletin, probably very non-committal but Angela might guess, might with hindsight read a lot into that recall from leave with all its overtones of urgency and sudden operations. What would it be? *The Admiralty has announced a raid on the French coast . . . it is feared there have been casualties.* Something like that would be the usual style. They wouldn't say right out that it had all been a bloody great flop and no one at all had returned; that would come out only a long while later, after the whole episode had been forgotten by the public. That was always the way of it. Of course, the families would be informed as soon as possible, but no details given. They would just have to mourn and wonder. Hope's fists clenched. *Why did nations have to fight each other?* In the end neither side got much out of it. Look at the Kaiser's Germany. Flat out in ruins, defeated in trying to win an empire, suffering roaring inflation and hunger, then along comes Hitler and turns them into virtual victors to start the whole thing going again while Britain gets trade depression and unemployment.

It was senseless.

Cusson said, 'What was that?'

'I didn't hear anything.'

'Sewer manhole, sir. Listen. Hear it now?'

Hope did; there was a man descending the ladder. Octavius

159

heard it too, and came along with his automatic rifle. They waited; they saw the man, saw the heavy rubber kneeboots coming down rung by rung. He reached the bottom and turned. He was a big man, bearded, wearing a tough-looking hip-length coat. Octavius held out a hand. 'Jean-Max,' he said, '*mon ami!* What is going on in Brest above us?'

The bearded man showed a line of teeth. 'Confusion – I do not know,' he said, spreading heavily gloved hands. 'It is bad, I think . . . but we carry on, we the *maquis*. You wish to be taken to the commandos, I am told. Which is the British Naval officer?'

'I am,' Hope said.

The man looked him up and down, playing his own torch on his face for a moment. 'I shall assist,' he said shortly. 'You will come with me. It will be dangerous for us all.'

He said no more. He turned away, giving an abrupt gesture for the party to follow. Octavius went immediately behind him, then Hope and Leading Seaman Cusson and the mixed bag of *maquis* and disguised Naval ratings. It was an eerie procession, only dimly lit by the torches, along the raised platform above the foul-smelling water, deeper and deeper into the constriction of the sewer's rotting brickwork. In places the platform seemed to descend and before it rose again the water slopped over and they moved through horrible matter and an increased smell that almost took their breath away. More reverberations came from above, some of them heavier than before. Shells – the port was taking a pounding. Hope said, 'I suppose it's *Probity*.' Cusson had another explanation to offer.

'That support ship, sir. The one the Bible signal was from. Could be her, coming up the Goulet. Something heavier than the old *Probity*'s got if you ask me.'

They moved on. The way seemed endless. Cusson wondered what his mum would think if she could see him now, wading through – what he was wading through. French at that, it didn't bear thinking about. He was surprised, really, that the French had got around to sewers, he'd always heard that they used *pissoirs* and holes in the ground. But no doubt even they had to connect with a sewage system . . . In the torchlight now and again he could see dead things – mice, rats, even cats. God knew how they got there. And the stench: he wouldn't survive this for much longer; all around him the lads were retching their guts up and the officer had gone green. What with all this and the bombings and slaughter back in the southern part of the Rade de Brest they'd had a real go of it, no joking. And the end result? What he'd said to subby – a POW camp and mouldering away till Hitler was no more. The notion of Hitler winning didn't enter his head. Right from the start the Navy had known they were going to lick the sod. The whole country knew it, in fact. Never lost a war except to the Yanks and on that occasion the British hadn't really got a good cause to fight, which made a difference. Also, they hadn't got Churchill then.

Even down there in the sewer Leading Seaman Cusson had no doubts about the final outcome. Just his own personal outcome was at stake, his and the rest of the filth-covered party.

Above ground in the Goulet Archer had reached the forebridge. By this time the oncoming ship was in sight and had been identified as a 6-inch-gun cruiser. Archer asked, 'Do we continue out, sir?'

'Yes, Number One.'

Archer felt relief but was careful not to let it show. The relief took a knock when Cameron, finishing the taking of a bearing on Petit Minou, went on. He said, 'I'm not risking a turn just here. When we're in wider water I'll come round into her wake and go back in. All right?'

'All right,' Archer said. 'Still going to do a torpedo run?'

'That's the idea.'

Archer said, 'It's a bloody daft one. I never thought it would come off. Now it hasn't a chance. The Nazis have got everything but the kitchen sink outside the entry to the pens.'

'I'm still going to try it, Number One.'

'But – look, it's crazy – '

Cameron said crisply, 'I suggest you keep your thoughts to yourself, Number One.'

'I think it's time someone spoke out.' Archer's voice was high.

'Now you've done so. Your comments are noted. If you wish they'll be logged. But in the meantime you'll obey my orders, and one of them is this: no more questioning of what I've decided to do. If you say anything further about it, it's your name that will be entered in the log for insubordinate conduct during action. Do I make myself clear, Number One?'

Archer muttered something and turned away. He went down the ladder. Cameron forced him from his mind. By now the gunfire was being concentrated on the cruiser and *Probity* was being left alone for the time being. As the two ships passed close Cameron used his loud hailer, directing it on to the cruiser's bridge. He called across, 'Senior Officer Operation Scatter . . . I propose turning shortly and following you in. I have men still ashore.'

In the back-glow from the gunfire and the flames that were starting along the shore as the 6-inch guns crashed out Cameron saw a cap waved from the bridge in acknowledgement. The cruiser swept on through the Goulet, taking pilotage risks, her wash streaming back. As soon as it was safe to do so, Cameron passed down the orders to bring *Probity* round. With her helm hard-a-starboard, port engine moving ahead and starboard engine astern, the destroyer turned short round, heeling sharply over so that the water rose up around her port side, coming inboard by the torpedo-tubes and swirling around the gunner's seaboots. As *Probity* steadied, once again on an inward course, another shore explosion was seen away ahead in the port area, apparently on the far side of the U-boat shelters. Not as huge as the earlier one farther east, but big. Cameron brought up his binoculars: fire had broken out – one of the cruiser's shells had probably taken something in the dockyard – and was blazing furiously. Some warehouse, perhaps . . . in the brilliant light Cameron saw that whatever it was it wasn't the bomb-proof shelters which were standing as solidly as before, totally unscathed.

Probity raced on.

15

The bearded man, the new guide addressed
by Octavius as Jean-Max, halted the party in the sewer as the
explosion happened right above them.

It seemed like the end; or very close to it.

The sewer appeared to lift bodily, in an upwards and
sideways movement, then to rock. Fumes filled the air; the
water-level rose and stinking liquid, sludgy and thick, washed
over the men to waist level. The torches were still giving light;
in that light Hope saw smoke wreathing back on them from
ahead, and in the smoke he believed he saw the flicker of
flame. Even to breathe was already becoming difficult; his
lungs felt on fire, and everywhere men began to choke,
rasping at their throats.

Jean-Max was calling out reassuringly. 'Soon it will clear,'
he said in French and English. 'But damage has been done
and I do not yet know how much. I shall go ahead to look, and
you will all stay here.'

In the torchlight Hope saw the Frenchman move ahead and
lose himself in the smoke. The flicker of flame had died away
now. Hope looked round at Leading Seaman Cusson.
'Wonder what caused that,' he said in a taut voice.

'A bloody big bang,' Cusson said.

'Yes, but what?'

'No idea, sir. Unless the Jerries've decided to flush out the
commandos now things've started happening.'

'Blown their sector of the sewer?'

'Seems likely enough if you ask me.' Cusson sounded

impatient; it shouldn't be the officer who was asking the questions. Officers were supposed to know, or if they didn't they made out they did, which was often enough maddening but at times like this gave a sort of encouragement. Even when you knew they were talking through their hats . . . it showed they were at best stirring up their grey matter. Cusson knew that young subby didn't really know if he was on his arse or his elbow. No experience to fall back on – come to that, neither had any of them, not of bloody filthy Frog sewers.

They waited, keeping a torch switched on. It was a desperate feeling. After a while Hope began to shake like a leaf in a gale. Cusson looked at him, eyes narrowed. Panic? You couldn't blame him, not really. But he should have had some confidence in the Frenchy who'd gone on ahead and knew what he was talking about. Mind, he was taking his time . . . Cusson said, 'It'll be all right, sir. That Frog bloke said it would clear soon.'

Hope was panting for air, more than the rest of them were, clawing at his throat. He gasped out, 'I – I feel shut in. I feel I'm going mad.'

Cusson nodded. Claustrophobia they called it. Cusson knew about claustrophobia, he had an aunt who suffered from it, so badly she even left the bog door wide open . . . He said, 'Don't think about it, sir. Think about something else. Think about Pompey. All the pubs in Queen Street.' As soon as he'd said it he knew that Queen Street and its pubs wouldn't help much; officers drank in the Queen's Hotel – a different kettle of fish, down in Southsea, the posh part. Cusson had gone in there once and had been shown the door by a bloke in a gilded blue uniform, like a master-at-arms in fancy dress. Meanwhile subby was shaking more than ever.

'Take it easy,' Cusson said. 'It's the same for all of us. Me, I'd sooner be in cells in RNB and that's saying something. Ever seen the cells, have you?'

'No . . .' The voice was hysterical. 'I think we ought to

165

go back.'

'Go back where for Christ's sake?'

'Back to the ladder. The manhole.'

'I wouldn't do that if I was you, sir. That Frog knows the system. We got to rely on him or we're done for.'

'He won't come back,' Hope said. 'I know he won't. He's left us to it, or he's – '

'Now, now.' Cusson's voice was patient, as though talking to a child. 'Course he'll be back, don't you fret – ' He broke off as Hope made a sudden move to the rear, thrusting him aside so that he almost fell into the sludgy muck below. Before Cusson could grab him, he'd pushed through the men behind, really panicking now, striking out, breathing like a steam engine . . . Cusson shouted to the others to stop him and they did. Cusson moved through towards him. 'Come on, sir,' he said. 'Just snap out of it.'

Hope's eyes were blazing madly and his face in the torchlight was a deathly white. He wasn't going to snap out of it, that was obvious. What he needed was a hard slap across the face, but Cusson wasn't accustomed to striking officers. He felt a hand on his shoulder and turned to find Octavius there. The Resistance man understood. He said, 'I shall do what you cannot,' and took Hope across the face twice, once on each cheek. Hope looked astonished, and gave himself a shake. 'I am sorry,' Octavius said. There was no response from the sub-lieutenant but Cusson fancied there was an ashamed look and that meant that something had got through to him. Cusson blew out his breath in relief; but the relief didn't survive the nasty thought that they were still right up the creek and no paddle in sight. That Frenchy could have been nabbed by the Nazis . . . Cusson was thinking of this when there was a shout from behind him, from the direction taken by the Frenchy earlier, and he turned and saw a number of figures lurching out from the smoke in filthy uniforms of camouflaged khaki; and in the lead, not lurching but marching smartly as if on parade, came Colour-Sergeant Mather, Royal Marines.

Out in the Goulet Cameron saw no point in maintaining secrecy as to his intentions. It was now a case of win or lose it all; at this stage there was no further protection the Nazis could mount against a torpedo attack, and the cruiser, now identified as HMS *Glamorgan*, had to be informed of what he meant to do. He passed the order to *Probity*'s leading signalman, now acting yeoman, to call up *Glamorgan* by light. *Glamorgan* was to be asked to continue ahead past the U-boat shelters and clear the channel for *Probity*'s entry on a torpedo firing run.

Quickly the reply came back: *Will do.*

Cameron set his teeth and braced himself with his hands on the binnacle, arms at full stretch, as the destroyer moved on, back into the gunfire that criss-crossed the port like music-hall swords piercing the woman in the cabinet. They couldn't live through it for long enough, couldn't possibly . . . with every ounce of his strength, with all his determination, Cameron willed his ship to success, willed her to remain afloat until Cantley had fired off his tin fish. Down by the tubes, Mr Cantley was doing much the same thing with an additional prayer to the Almighty – that he might be lent, just for long enough, the skill to fire the bloody things without making a monkey's fist of it. Not being a gunner(T) he didn't feel all that confident. He lacked the experience. Same with Petty Officer Todd. Guns were one thing, torpedoes another, Todd reckoned, and as a gunnery man he didn't go much on them, although he was prepared to admit that if and when they hit their targets they caused a bloody sight more destruction than did most guns, a sight more in fact than *Glamorgan*'s 6-inch turrets. But torpedoes hissed and plopped where guns gave a nice healthy bang. Torpedoes had minds of their own, independent of gunner's mates. Projies went where you aimed them, torpedoes didn't, not always. They could be thrown off course by undisciplined extraneous things like eddies and currents or by something going wrong with their propulsion apparatus. If you were a torpedo-gunner's mate . . . anyway, to hell with it, Todd thought as the destroyer moved on past the flashes and the shells wanged away over their heads, they did have that LTO, Ledger. He should know enough to fill in where the gunnery brains left off.

If he didn't get flattened by a projy first. God, Todd thought, was certainly with them tonight or they'd have gone long ago. He hoped God could keep it up, not get waylaid by some request from elsewhere, like from the German command . . . but Todd refused to believe that the Nazis were God's children. It ought to be all right. But you did need faith. Todd, rather late in life, told God that he had faith. Even in his own ears, however, it sounded like an OD's daft excuse for crime when up before the other God at Captain's Defaulters . . .

As Todd thought about assistance from heaven, Sub-Lieutenant Hope, across the harbour and still below the streets of the port, was approached by Colour-Sergeant Mather who had enquired who was the officer in charge from *Palatine*. He had already been informed as to the course of events by Jean-Max. Now, he marched up to Hope, outlined in the light from the torches, disturbing the sludge as he halted with an attempt at slammed boots, and saluted smartly.

'Sir! Colour-Sergeant Mather, sir, reporting with twenty-eight Royal Marine commandos. Released into the main sewer by force of that explosion. Major Shawcross and all other officers dead, leaving me in command of the detachment. Sir!'

In the ambience of the sewer it was almost grotesque. Cusson grinned to himself as the sub-lieutenant returned the salute, but he knew you had to admire it.

Hope said, 'Thank you, Colour-Sergeant.' He seemed, Cusson thought, uncertain what to say next, but it didn't matter since Mather said it for him.

'Permission to re-mount the assault on the U-boat shelters, sir.'

'I'm – '

168

'There is a way out to the fresh air, sir, and there is a way into the purlieus of the shelters, sir.'

'But – '

'And I have enough of the explosive charges to be effective, sir.' Mather unbent for a moment, his blackened face creasing into a devilish grin. 'We're not bloody beaten, sir. Not yet, sir. And never will be. Sir!'

The emphatic 'Sir!' seemed to bring Mather's remarks to a conclusion. Hope could now get a word in. He said, 'I'm sorry, Colour-Sergeant. My Captain's coming in with *Probity*. He intends to fire off torpedoes.'

Mather gaped, taken off balance at last. 'Fire 'em into the pens, sir?'

'Yes – '

'Strike a bleeding light, begging your pardon, sir.' Mather wiped sweat and filth from his face. 'How long before Lieutenant-Commander Cameron fires off the fish, sir?'

Hope said, 'I don't know. But it'll be soon.'

'In that case, sir,' Mather said, 'we'd best make haste. Upwards. I don't know if you know it or not, sir, but we're hard alongside the shelters, where we are now.'

Hope nodded. He asked, 'Where's that Resistance man now? Jean-Max?'

Cusson said, 'Coming back now, sir.' He pointed towards the smoke, which was thinning at last. Jean-Max called out and gestured them all to follow him. He turned back without more delay; Cusson got the Naval party on the move and with the men of the *maquis* they wallowed through the sewer water, stumbling about as they met shattered brickwork, falls of the wall brought about by that last heavy explosion, with the bare earth showing up in places as the torches flickered, earth that broke away bit by bit and dropped into the foul water to bring it up in spouts that spattered the party below. They had just cleared one section when there was something like a landslide behind them, loud and threatening. Cusson looked back. 'Never see that end again,' he observed. 'Talk about a total blockage!'

Hope, face set, moved on as fast as he could go. He looked at his wrist-watch: he was astonished to find it showed only a little after 2100. He felt he had been down in the sewer for a lifetime. And he wasn't out yet. Feelings of panic arose again. At any moment now *Probity*, if all was going to plan above, would be going into her firing run. By now, they could hear the constant sound of the guns overhead: they gave Hope some confidence again. It must surely mean they were in contact with the fresh air, that the lifeline was still open – ahead at any rate. It was something to cling to. But the chances were that when they did emerge it would be into Nazi hands.

It was only seconds later that all hope died. Jean-Max, who had gone on well ahead of the rest, came back, stumbling in his haste. His face was grey in the light from his torch. He said, 'There has been a fall of brick and earth ahead. There is now no way out.'

Cusson felt light-headed. But he pulled himself together fast and said, 'We can always dig. Or try to. With out hands. How about the air?'

Jean-Max wrung his hands. He said, 'The air will last a little while. Not long.'

'Anyone know we're here? Your lot, I mean, the Resistance?'

'Yes,' Jean-Max said. His tone seemed to indicate that it was already too late. A moment later he spoke again, underlining the hopelessness. He said, 'They will try to warn the British ships. But I do not think that will help us.'

Cusson's breath hissed out between his teeth. The torpedoes might be a better death. Certainly a faster one. He looked at the officer: Hope was in a bad way. Soon, they all would be. Might as well have opted for the submarine service, Cusson thought, and got the extra pay. But he'd never fancied lying helpless on the sea bottom, being depth-charged. Which was much like what they were facing now. Cusson's mind reeled – light-headed again. He reached out a hand and

Hope's shoulder. He said, 'Don't worry, it may never happen.' Bloody trite, he thought, but still. He couldn't think of anything else to say. Hope put his head in his hands. Cusson left him and started walking along ahead, towards the earth fall reported by Jean-Max. The Frenchman watched him go, and shrugged. He would see for himself, the English sailor would. Cusson did. When he reached the fall, he tore and ripped with his bare hands. He was joined by several more men. All they got was torn-out fingernails and a lot of blood. The earth was solid, hard packed and wet, mixed with the bricks.

'Bloody hopeless,' Cusson said savagely. But they went on because it was better to be doing something while the air lasted than sit around and do nothing.

In the open air, not so much fresh now as filled with the stench of cordite and gunsmoke, the message was being passed to the British destroyer, passed by light from a brave man willing to risk his life from high up in a tall house overlooking the harbour. The message, passed slowly in English, was read off by Cameron's leading signalman.

'Light flashing from the shore, sir. British persons blocked in sewer close to U-boat shelters.'

Cameron was shaken. 'No indication of how many?'

'No, sir. Call the sender back, sir?'

'No! That'd put him at more risk.' Cameron was a prey to indecision. By now he was not far off the entry to the pens, past the docks where the commandos had been put ashore originally, and his ship was still in good enough shape to go into the attack though the upperworks looked as if they were held together only by the remaining paint. His radar had been shot away, the HA gun admidships had been taken bodily by an exploding shell, the mainmast and the searchlight platform had gone, the whaler was in fragments, but two of the 4-inch guns were still in action, firing fast and doing damage to the shore gun batteries and the waterfront buildings. Ahead of him *Glamorgan* was blasting through towards the northern

171

arm of the Rade and already her main armament had despatched both the German frigates that had been lying off the pens. They would now be pilotage hazards but nothing more.

The stage was set; all was ready and the objective of Operation Scatter stood a chance, by a miracle, of succeeding. *Glamorgan* had made sacrifices already: Cameron had seen that she had taken some hits and there would be many casualties aboard her. *Probity* had suffered further casualties as well, far too many. Could all that sacrifice be thrown away? Or should he think of the men entombed in the horror of the sewers, and call it a day – back out, inform *Glamorgan* that it had all been wasted and that she had better fight back through to the Goulet as best she could, and withdraw with nothing whatsoever achieved?

'Can't be done,' he said aloud, and then realized that Archer had come to the bridge.

Archer asked, 'What can't be done, sir?'

Cameron told him. 'Even if I did . . . the chances are those men wouldn't be got out by the Nazis. Easier for them to leave them where they are.' His thoughts followed those of Leading Seaman Cusson. 'Torpedoes might be better.'

'Whichever way it's to be,' Archer said, 'it's got to be decided fast. In seconds.'

Cameron said quietly, 'Yes, I know.' A surge of helplessness rose in him, a hatred of the war and the decisions that a commanding officer was forced into, decisions that either killed or did not kill men who relied upon him to make the right ones. *Even if the right ones were the lethal ones?* Inside himself he knew very well which was the right one in this case, which the Admiralty would consider the right one too. But he wanted, above all in this moment of agony, to be able to say to Archer, Come on, Number One, stop sounding antagonistic and unfriendly and just tell me your own thoughts and feelings, what you would do if you were in command . . . But he knew, of course, that he could never do that, could never

172

press anyone to share, to be half responsible. A captain had to do his own job.

He said, 'Carry on as ordered, Number One.'

'Aye, aye, sir,' Archer answered flatly.

Cameron looked aft, across the shatter of his upperworks that gave him a clear view of the triple mountings of the tubes to port and starboard, at Cantley and the gunner's mate waiting for his word. By this time the communication system was a shambles and there was no contact with the tubes other than by word of mouth. Cameron resumed his forward-looking position and watched for the entry to the pens, great bastions of stone some eighty feet apart, to loom up into the firing position.

His mouth dry and his heart like lead, he passed the order ninety seconds later. 'Stand by torpedo-tubes.'

Archer repeated it in a shout down to the upper deck: *'Stand by torpedo-tubes!'*

Cantley and Todd acknowledged. The gunner would be the first to fire; then, if necessary, Todd on the return run. Neither of them would know they were firing at British personnel and Resistance men. Not till afterwards. For now, they were lucky, Cameron thought as his fingers gripped the azimuth circle on the binnacle, gripped till the knuckles showed white in the gun flashes. Below, Mr Cantley's finger was ready on the firing button and his eyes were narrowed as though sheer concentration would ensure that his tin fish ran straight and true, right into the heart of the half-built complex, and send the whole issue sky high for good and all, and maybe a good deal of Brest with it, which wouldn't please Whitehall. He was sorry for the innocent inhabitants, so many of them Gaullists, but war was war and he was there to protect British lives, the merchant seamen who sailed in the convoys that brought food and the sinews of war to Britain, the men of the escorts who fought those convoys through against the German aircraft and U-boats. Deny the bastards a safe base and as the skipper had said, their range would be very nicely cut and the convoys would be at much less risk.

173

On the bridge, Cameron, watching closely, was about to cut his speed by putting his engines briefly astern, thus giving the torpedoes a better chance as he came abeam of the entry, when there was a light step on the ladder and Marie Chalandon appeared.

16

Glamorgan had done her work well: the gunfire from opposite the pens had ceased now; as the heavy cruiser rushed on, her stem made glancing contact with the nearer German frigate, already well down by the head. The sinking ship was nudged over to starboard, giving *Probity* a clear run through, with room beyond to make a tight turn for her second attack. Cameron heard the girl's voice just as he called the wheelhouse.

'Captain, please – '

'Not now!'

She came up to him. 'I read the message, the light. Please do not fire! There is a better way.'

Cameron shook her off. It was now or never. Down the voice-pipe he said, 'Both engines full astern.' The response was immediate; the way came off sharply. Thirty seconds later *Probity* was off the entry, drifting slowly ahead with engines stopped now, her bows coming up past the western mole. Cameron nodded at Archer.

The First Lieutenant shouted the order down: 'Port tubes, fire when ready!'

Cantley's reaction was instant. *Fire one, fire two, fire three . . .* There was a hiss as the tin fish ran out, a plopping sound as they took the water. Their courses could be seen just beneath the surface, tons of HE moving through towards the shelters. Cameron held his breath. Below, Cantley and Todd did the same. As the last of the torpedoes passed through between the defences dead on target Cameron put his engines to full ahead. Within seconds there was an explosion, and a mountain of water rose up to port. All along *Probity*'s decks the depleted ship's company watched the start of a lick of flame, heard the crash of masonry. And listened for two more explosions.

They didn't come.

Cantley swore viciously. 'Bastards. One's going to be sod all bloody use!' Already the bridge was shouting down, asking questions. Number One . . . Cantley snapped back, 'I don't bloody know but I'll be finding out. Call it bloody temperament!'

Probity moved on past the entry. Ahead, *Glamorgan* was slowing preparatory to making her turn for the run back towards the Goulet. There was a good deal of confusion ashore, and a searchlight probed around again, outlining the two British ships. In its back-glow Cameron could see German troops around the shelters, men running hither and thither in an obvious state of panic. There was so far no more gunfire. Cameron thought of the men in the sewer: they kept intruding. He was aware of Marie Chalandon talking in a low voice to Archer. It was Archer who approached him.

'The girl's asking you not to fire off any more fish, sir.'

'What's the alternative, Number One? Her alternative, I mean.'

Archer said, 'She wants those men out first.'

'Who doesn't?' Cameron's voice was bitter.

'She says she can do it. I reckon it's not too late – just the one torpedo won't have done all that amount of damage and they may be all right. She's wanted by the Germans, wanted badly. Don't you see?'

'A hostage?'

'Of a sort, yes. She's offering to trade herself for the release of the men in the sewers – '

'They'd just drop right into German hands.'

'She thinks that's better than dying in the sewer. And I agree.'

Cameron asked, 'Is this a case of a boyfriend, Number

176

One? Someone in Brest she doesn't – '

'She didn't say so, sir. I doubt it. She wouldn't have wanted to go to England leaving a boyfriend behind, I imagine.'

Cameron swung round on the girl. 'Is it, Marie? And what about your mother?'

She said, 'It is all of them. Your sailors, and my friends of the *maquis*. My mother, she will go to England with you and be safe.' Her faith in the British Navy was total. 'That is all I want. I am willing to stay.'

'You think the Germans'll dig those men out, and leave us and the *Glamorgan* here in the meantime, threatening – '

'Yes,' she said defiantly. 'If you send a message to the German military commander, telling him what I have suggested. A truce only, until I am on the shore and the men dug out.' She looked back at him steadily. He passed a hand across his face. Her suggestion was full of holes, couldn't be taken seriously. No such exchange could possibly be made, neither side would trust the other. But the offer having been made it had to be considered. And then rejected. Cameron could never bring himself to hand over the girl to the bestialities of the Gestapo, just to mention one aspect. But he still shrank from what he had to do, what he might already have done, to the entombed men ashore, so close . . .

He stiffened himself. 'The answer's no,' he said flatly. 'You could never have expected me to say anything else, Marie.'

She looked at him, her eyes blazing in the continuing flames from the shore. Then she turned on her heel and went down the ladder. Cameron, conning the destroyer on towards where the *Glamorgan* was now turning, thrust the girl from his mind. Down the voice-pipe he said, 'Both engines half ahead.' Forty-five seconds later he was abeam of the cruiser, now on the reciprocal of her inward course. He passed the orders to bring his own ship round. 'Full ahead port engine, full astern starboard, wheel hard-a-starboard.'

Probity's stern swung out to port. Cameron said, 'Stand by torpedoes.'

In the sewer's terrible constriction, in the fetid air that was fast being used up, the explosion of the one torpedo had come shatteringly. There had been a fierce upward surge of the earth, as though the force of the explosion had travelled beneath them. There was a roaring sound that seemed to go on and on. When at last the earth steadied many of the men had been buried deep, never to be got at again. Leading Seaman Cusson, shaking in every limb, found himself alive. Just about. Close to him the sub-lieutenant lay with his head crushed in, probably by a fall of brickwork or stone. Cusson couldn't see this, all the torches had gone now, but he could feel it when he groped around in the pitch darkness.

A sticky mess, like a broken egg, at the end of a neck. A collar and tie . . . the officer was the only one with a collar and tie. Here and there men were crying out, in agony, in terror. Cusson shouted out, letting them know someone else was alive and capable of speech. Of motion, too. Cusson felt his body, moved his limbs. He was functioning.

He pulled himself to his feet. There was room to stand up.

He felt very shaky and unco-ordinated, not fully in control of his movements. He staggered, fell, got up again. He heard sounds of other movement. After a moment the Frenchy, Octavius, identified himself away to Cusson's left. Then some more.

Cusson said, 'One explosion, I reckon. Anyone hear any others?'

No one had, but it wasn't conclusive: none of them had been thinking about how many, not consciously.

Cusson moved instinctively towards where he had heard Octavius. Octavius was the leader of the Frenchies . . . bugger all he could do now, but just the same, you might as well die in good company. There had been no fear in Octavius, all the way along.

Cusson reached him. 'Looks like the end now, mate. Won't be prolonged, that's one thing. The skipper, he'll be back in soon. Second run.'

'Yes,' Octavius said. He said no more than that; Cusson got

the idea he was praying. Cusson prayed too, fervently; they said it was never too late; on the other hand there was always an opposite saying, and the one that came to mind now was, it's later than you think.

Irritably Cusson dabbed a hand at his face, which was starting to feel wet. That bloody sewage, dripping on him. Then he realized that it wasn't sewage, it was rain. What a bloody time for the perishing rain to come back. Might just as well be Easter Monday back in Pompey . . .

Rain. *It was bloody raining!* Cusson looked up. He couldn't see any sky, but that didn't mean it wasn't there. But there was light – fires. He yelled it out: 'We've been shoved up! We're not all that far from the surface!'

It came blindingly then: they could get out with luck, and they would have to do it fast. He knew they were not far from the water. Quickly he began organizing. There were quite a few men who could move. They would have to carry out those who couldn't.

The light from above was increasing, the fires spreading no doubt. The air was freshening fast. Looking up, Cusson saw that the gap above was widening as more earth and bricks fell away, showering down with a clatter of rubble. Nature – nature given a hard thrust by that last explosion – was doing their work for them. Now Cusson could see who was alive and kicking. 'You and you and you,' he said, once again the leading seaman with hope for a future. 'Smack it about, take the wounded with us, all right? Soon as we're up and out, we make a dash for the water and watch out for Jerries . . .'

Probity had made her turn and was steadying for the final act when the girl dived overboard from aft and began swimming fast for the shore just eastward of the pens. Archer saw her go, and reported.

Cameron felt sick. What the girl faced now . . . he said, 'For God's sake. At this stage! What made her do that?'

Archer said, 'Your refusal, I'd say, sir.'

'Thank you, Number One. I don't see what she hopes to

179

achieve.'

Archer tapped his forehead meaningly. 'Round the bend. She's been under strain.'

'Either that or she couldn't in the end face leaving all those Resistance men to it, mother or no mother. Saw herself as running out on them. I don't suppose we'll ever know now.' Cameron watched the U-boat shelters as the destroyer made her approach once again. There had been some damage he believed, a reinforced wall was leaning drunkenly, but it would be repairable. Any moment now . . . already he had reduced his speed. Ahead of him *Glamorgan* opened suddenly with her main armament, all her remaining 6-inch guns in action, pumping the projectiles into the port and its defences, softening-up, sending the shells from one turret into the shelters in advance of the torpedoes. Standing ready at the starboard triple mounting, Petty Officer Todd watched the scene appreciatively.

'Give the buggers hell,' he remarked to the LTO.

'You can say that again, GI.' Leading Torpedoman Ledger had suffered from the Jerries more than once and had lost a brother serving in the Northern Patrol at the start of the war. He spat on his hands, waiting the moment when his torpedoes would finish the job. That Cantley was still moaning about the two that hadn't gone off, but maybe he'd stop when the next three went in – always assuming they blew, of course. Ledger believed they would. They couldn't have another go of rotten luck. And the good old *Glamorgan* was causing some nice, preliminary havoc ashore. Ledger didn't suppose the Jerries had ever imagined they would see a British cruiser blasting close-quarter hell out of Brest . . .

The heavy gunfire was assisting Cusson and his party as well. Scrambling from the sewer's wreckage, carrying the unfit men between them, they found total chaos and an immense amount of damage – and no German troops. Climbing over the piles of rubble, slipping and sliding, they made the waterside in good order: and that was when Cusson saw the girl. He recognized her as she came out of the water,

180

and he ran for her.

'Funny place to find you,' he said. 'What's the idea, eh?'

She gave him a scared look, then dodged aside, avoiding his outstretched arm. She ran to the rear, looking about, searching the faces of the remnant of the Resistance men. She found Octavius not far behind Cusson. Cusson heard her say something in French heard her call back in English: 'There is a boat, Englishman – '

Cusson ran ahead to the broken wall. True enough, there was a boat, a biggish one with a motor, secured to ring-bolts in the wall. One of the ring-bolts had been broken away during the gunfire earlier. Cusson shouted to the men to close in behind him, then he went over the wall, dropping down into the harbour, and clambered aboard the boat. He shouted up again, telling the men to jump. As he did so there was a burst of machine-gun fire from above, a burst at close range that virtually blew those that had been hit over the wall into the water. One of them was Marie Chalandon. She took the water and floated, head down, arms outspread. The rest of the men, the fit and the wounded, not so many left now, jumped into the water and swam for the boat. Cusson looked up; on the lip of the wall Colour-Sergeant Mather stood, firing a sub-machine-gun from the hip, spraying from left to right and back again before he fell to one knee with a line of bullets down his right side. Amazingly he fired another burst, then toppled over, legs and arms slack. There was no more firing. As the boat filled with the survivors, Cusson started the engine, cut the remaining rope with his seaman's knife, and headed out for *Probity* in the overladen craft.

From the bridge Cameron saw them. From the torpedo tubes Mr Cantley and Petty Officer Todd also saw them. It was Todd who shouted the warning to the hands on the after 4-inch:

'Stand by to pass a line, there!'

Then the firing order came down from Cameron and was obeyed on the instant by the gunner's mate. The three torpedoes emerged, dropped, as before went true on course for the entrance to the pens. As before Todd held his breath. Cantley had crossed over from port to starboard to watch. As the explosions came all hands ducked into such cover as they could find. It was a fantastic sight, and it came just as Cusson's boat was being cast a line by Stripey Trudge. A blast of flame and heat: all three torpedoes, this time, had found their mark. The scene was lit like day. Todd had a feeling that even the two dud fish had gone up in the massive uprush of the explosions. Chunks of masonry were hurled into the air, many of them coming down dangerously close to *Probity*'s starboard side where Cusson had taken the line from Trudge and was turning it up around a cleat in the fore part of the boat to be towed along by the destroyer.

Probity moved on; Cameron, with his engines to full ahead, followed past the dereliction of the shelters and the port in *Glamorgan*'s wake. The shore was silent, or almost. From the starboard side a solitary battery opened uselessly; the wind of its shells was heard passing astern. Behind them now, smoke billowed out, thick and black along a rising wind. The sky was lit with orange and red as the fires blazed behind the ships, thundering at full power down the Goulet.

As Petit Minou was left away to starboard, Cameron called the w/t office. 'Bridge,' he said. 'Make to Admiralty in plain language: *Operation Scatter, objective achieved.*

Off Lundy, HMS *Glamorgan* parted company, swinging away up the Irish Sea for the Firth of Clyde. *Probity*, all that was left now, turned to starboard up the Bristol Channel. Little more than thirty-six hours after leaving Barry she was lying off the lock and awaiting the tide. Awaiting extensive repairs as well . . . Cameron, as he rang off the engines, looked along his decks. So many men dead, so many wounded, his own ship left behind, a wreck in the Rade de Brest. John Grey, captain of *Probity* until he had been so badly wounded, was still alive and still unconscious. He had already been transferred to hospital, put aboard a boat that had come out from the army's ordnance depot at Sully. He might yet live, but it was doubtful. Chief Petty Officer King was alive and fit; but Bartlett had died as they had made their dash out from the Goulet, almost cut in half by a sliver of steel torn off by the last German shell to hit the ship.

Had the objective been worthwhile? Cameron was dead tired, nearly out on his feet, and that made the feeling of depression worse. He met Archer's eye. He said, 'Well, Number One. You can say it if you like: I told you so – that was it, wasn't it?'

'I don't think so, sir. We brought if off, didn't we? Or you did.'

'We all did. I dare say it's done some good. There's a lot of families who aren't going to think so, though. In France as well as UK. Where's Octavius?'

Archer said, 'Below, sir. Comforting the old lady . . . Mme Chalandon. Husband and daughter both gone within hours – it's tough, all right.'

Cameron asked, 'Have you spoken to him?'

'Octavius – about Marie? Yes, I have.' Archer took a long look at the Barry shore, at the docks, away towards Sully Island, back westerly again to Barry Island, pre-war resort of the holidaymakers from the grim valleys to the north. It all looked peaceful: it was a bright day, filled with sunshine, very different from what they'd left behind in Brest. He said, 'The girl spoke to him just before the Nazis got her. What we thought – that was the fact: she didn't fancy running out and leaving all those men to it. But when she heard that all who could be got out of the sewer *had* been got out . . . well, then she wanted to rejoin her mother and come across to England. Pity she never made it – after all she did for us.'

Cameron felt dead inside, as he had felt on previous occasions during the attack. He turned away and went below, leaving the ship to his First Lieutenant. From the upper deck Stripey Trudge saw him come down the ladder – like a zombie, Trudge thought. They'd all had a bad time and the skipper had carried the whole weight almost from the start. Stripey had a moment's flash of insight into the demands made on officers by responsibility – it was showing in the skipper's face. Stripey was amazed that any of them had come through. He gave himself a pinch all over: he was there all right, safe and sound. One thing: he'd laid the ghost of his old dad's premonitions.